P9-CDL-601

—THE **TOYOTA WAY**——
ᵀᴼ HEALTHCARE
EXCELLENCE

**American College of Healthcare Executives
Management Series Editorial Board**

John M. Snyder, FACHE
Carle Foundation Hospital, Urbana, IL

Lynn I. Boggs, FACHE
Presbyterian Health/Novant, Charlotte, NC

Ronald A. Charles, M.D.
Total Carolina Care, Columbia, SC

Ralph Charlip, FACHE
VA Health Administration Center, Denver, CO

Dennis E. Franks, FACHE
Neosho Memorial Regional Medical Center, Chanute, KS

Emily Y. Holliman, FACHE
Central Mississippi Medical Center, Jackson, MS

Kristin L. Schmidt, R.N., FACHE
Arizona Spine & Joint Hospital, Mesa, AZ

Kimberly K. Sharp
HCA, Nashville, TN

CDR Mark J. Stevenson, FACHE
TRICARE Regional Office, West Aurora, CO

Donald B. Wagner, LFACHE
Consultant, Sugar Land, TX

Fredrick C. Young, Jr, FACHE
Methodist Health System Foundation, Slidell, LA

—THE **TOYOTA WAY**————
TO HEALTHCARE
EXCELLENCE

INCREASE EFFICIENCY AND IMPROVE QUALITY WITH LEAN

John Black with
David Miller

ACHE Management Series

Your board, staff, or clients may also benefit from this book's insight. For more information on quantity discounts, contact the Health Administration Press Marketing Manager at (312) 424-9470.

This publication is intended to provide accurate and authoritative information in regard to the subject matter covered. It is sold, or otherwise provided, with the understanding that the publisher is not engaged in rendering professional services. If professional advice or other expert assistance is required, the services of a competent professional should be sought.

The statements and opinions contained in this book are strictly those of the author(s) and do not represent the official positions of the American College of Healthcare Executives or of the Foundation of the American College of Healthcare Executives.

Copyright © 2008 by the Foundation of the American College of Healthcare Executives. Printed in the United States of America. All rights reserved. This book or parts thereof may not be reproduced in any form without written permission of the publisher.

12 11 10 09 08   5 4 3 2 1

Library of Congress Cataloging-in-Publication Data

Black, John R.
  The Toyota way to healthcare excellence : increase efficiency and improve quality with Lean / John Black with David Miller.
    p. ; cm.
  Includes bibliographical references and index.
  ISBN-13: 978-1-56793-293-5 (alk. paper)
  ISBN-10: 1-56793-293-2 (alk. paper)
  1. Medical care—United States—Quality control. 2. Medical care—United States—Cost effectiveness. 3. Health services administration—United States. 4. Chief executive officers—United States. 5. Hospital administrators—United States. 6. Organizational effectiveness—United States. I. Miller, David, 1944 June 18- II. Title.
  [DNLM: 1. Health Facilities—organization & administration—United States. 2. Efficiency, Organizational—United States. 3. Organizational Innovation—United States. 4. Quality Assurance, Health Care—methods—United States. WX 150 B627t 2008]
  RA399.A3B53 2008
  362.1068—dc22

                    2007046264

The paper used in this publication meets the minimum requirements of American National Standard for Information Sciences—Permanence of Paper for Printed Library Materials, ANSI Z39.48-1984. ∞ ™

Acquisitions editor: Audrey Kaufman; Project manager: Helen-Joy Lynerd; Layout editor: Scott R. Miller; Cover design: Scott R. Miller

Health Administration Press
A division of the Foundation of the
        American College of Healthcare Executives
1 North Franklin Street, Suite 1700
Chicago, IL 60606-3529
(312) 424-2800

*This book is dedicated to all the people of this world who are now—
or who will become—patients. You come asking only for what you
have the right to receive. You expect safe, compassionate care provided
by healthcare professionals who make the elimination of waste and
defects a daily priority. You expect treatment with no fear of your condition being worsened from the procedures or medications provided,
to experience no avoidable uncertainties or concerns, and to be
treated as a respected and valued human being. In other words, you
have the right to all the benefits of Lean and the Toyota Production
System as applied to healthcare.*

John Black (center) with Virginia Mason Medical Center CEO Gary Kaplan (left) and former president Mike Rona at the Hitachi factory in Shizuoka, Japan, after just completing a *kaizen* event with a team from Virginia Mason.

Contents

Foreword

I FIRST HEARD about John Black and his pioneering Lean work at Boeing from Mike Rona, at that time my colleague and president of Virginia Mason Medical Center. Mike had met John on an airplane and was very impressed. He said, "You really have to meet this guy!"

At the time, Mike and I were becoming increasingly aware of quality and safety issues in healthcare and realized that errors were actually occurring at Virginia Mason as well. While all of us at Virginia Mason cared deeply about our "customers" (i.e., our patients) and took great pride in the quality of care at Virginia Mason, it was obvious to us that we could do so much better. The inefficient and ineffective processes prevalent in the healthcare industry were not designed to give our patients what they expected and deserved.

We quickly came to realize that there were numerous defects in the care and service being delivered to our patients. They waited too long for treatment, traveled too far in the hospital or clinic, and spent too much time going from place to place. Frankly, the care we and others in healthcare have been providing costs too much, to a great extent because of the waste inherent in the system (what Black calls "non–value-added"). Our processes have not been patient focused and have certainly not been focused on eliminating waste.

These realizations came at a time when we faced significant organizational challenges. Our economic performance was not as strong as required, and we needed to make great strides in quality and safety if we were to achieve our organizational aspirations. We were tired of feeling that we were "hanging on by our fingertips." We, the leaders and board at Virginia Mason, were ready to reenergize our mission and redefine our organizational vision. In a board-driven process, we created a new strategic plan predicated on the vision of becoming the quality leader in healthcare, not just in the Pacific Northwest, but in the world—an ambitious but worthy goal. The problem was that we didn't have a method—a management system—to make it happen.

Through the Toyota Production System (Lean), Black offered us a management system that focused on the customer, eliminated defects and waste, increased staff morale, and generated a margin. Each of these attributes clearly resonated with our leadership. The only problem: Lean had never been fully applied to healthcare. The question was, "Would a system that worked well for building automobiles work well for providing top-quality healthcare?"

As I listened to Black and read his book *A World Class Production System*, there was simply no question that every aspect of the Toyota Production System philosophy and methods applied to healthcare. Acceptable quality in both cases depended on defect-free processes. Black's compelling story and experience with and/or understanding of the application of Lean at Boeing, Genie-Terex, Wiremold, and other companies convinced Virginia Mason's leaders, including the board, that adopting Lean was the management method and optimal path for us to move forward.

Now, six years into our journey, the answer is clear. Lean is the management system Virginia Mason needed. We call our system, modified slightly to meet our own particular needs as a healthcare organization, the Virginia Mason Production System (VMPS). Despite some initial resistance to change—to be expected in any organization, but more so in healthcare with its long tradition of professional autonomy—VMPS is well established as a way of life at

Virginia Mason. We're past the tipping point and the results continue to be powerful in their positive impact for our patients and our staff.

Since beginning our implementation of VMPS, we've increased the number of patients treated each year while reducing the number of full-time employees required to treat them (through attrition, not layoffs). Our economic performance has stabilized, and patient and staff satisfaction have improved. In those service lines farthest along the path to full implementation of Lean ("model lines"), Virginia Mason has achieved dramatic reductions in the time patients spend waiting for and receiving care, the distance patients (and staff) travel to the treatment site, and, most importantly, medical errors (defects).

In healthcare, the worst defect is killing a patient. In 2004, we were well on our Lean journey when Mary McClinton came to Virginia Mason. Mary, a well-known and respected civic activist, died under our care due to an avoidable medical error. Virginia Mason's Patient Safety Alert System—based on what the Japanese call *jidoka* or "stop the line"—enabled us to immediately identify the cause of the error and prevent it from happening again. While tragically not in time to save Mary McClinton, this system encourages any employee at any time to halt any process if he or she believes something has gone wrong or might go wrong. At Virginia Mason, we call these stoppages "patient safety alerts." Mary's death at Virginia Mason was the darkest time in our history and has only spurred us on to go faster and work harder to build a defect-free—and therefore the safest—healthcare system for our patients.

In the following pages you'll be introduced to many new concepts, such as *takt* time (rate of demand), "just in time," and standard work. These concepts will seem foreign at first, but you'll find they're not that difficult to understand. Applying them rigorously, however, takes a great deal of leadership, commitment, time, and patience. Large-scale change is never easy or quick. The most important message I want to convey to you, however, is that Lean works!

You will face resistance as you implement Lean in your organization. This is inevitable, as all major change is met with resistance;

however, staying the course is worth it. Our patients are counting on us!

How do you combat resistance? It starts with the leader's deep commitment and perseverance. You will be tested over and over again. It has been critical that we not "blink" and that we consistently drive home the message that Lean is the organization's management system. We have to lead by example (for instance, by participating in the improvement processes or being on the "shop floor").

That also means evaluating and providing feedback to staff on their commitment to following Lean principles and practices. Some people will choose not to come along for the ride, and that's all right.

Finally, and most importantly, resistance tends to disappear when people see results that actually change their daily work lives and improve the patient experience. When people at Virginia Mason see the power of the Virginia Mason Production System by participating in Rapid Process Improvement Workshops (or "*kaizen* events") and are positively impacted by the results of these workshops, the momentum builds and resistance subsides.

Personally, I've learned through my own participation in Virginia Mason's many improvement activities how much waste was in the system and how frustrating many of our processes had become for our patients and our staff. I feel a deep accountability for these processes and now for their improvement. This means we must accelerate the application of *kaizen* (continuous incremental improvement) to processes throughout our organization.

Since Virginia Mason started on its Lean journey, we've conducted nearly 500 Rapid Process Improvement Workshops. Almost every one of them has led to significant improvements— at least a 50 percent reduction in time, space, or the need for other resources. In areas of major focus, we've seen defects go to nearly zero. We've experienced improvements in hospital length of stay, wait times to see a doctor, face-to-face time for patients with their physicians, time to get lab results, and even time to get the bill sent out. Lean works!

I encourage you to read this book with a great deal of attention and focus. Do not let the new terms or concepts deter you; use the glossary, but keep reading. Many of the answers to our healthcare challenges are right here. We can create a better, safer, more efficient, and higher-quality healthcare system if we are willing to embrace these new methods and are truly willing to lead.

Dr. Gary Kaplan
CEO, Virginia Mason Medical Center

PART I

INTRODUCTION

CHAPTER 1

An Open Letter to
Healthcare Leaders

WHEN I FIRST began consulting in 1999, after retiring with 21 years at Boeing and another 20 as an Army officer during the Cold War and Vietnam War, I was warned by consulting veterans to avoid three areas: government, education, and healthcare. Because these areas were so inwardly focused, they said, large-scale change would be a "nightmare." Furthermore, they added, "Healthcare as an industry is probably the least capable of changing because of its cottage-like struc-ture" (i.e., fragmented among many independent medical providers and facilities).

So, as I began my consulting work helping organizations suc-cessfully and profitably apply the Toyota Production System (TPS) model—often called "Lean production" or just "Lean"—to their own operations, I avoided these three areas. As fate would have it, how-ever, I happened to sit next to a farsighted healthcare president on a plane headed for Atlanta in October 2000. He became a captive audi-ence as I presented my laptop PowerPoint® presentation on Lean. He shared his enthusiasm with his boss, and he and I eventually got together and started Lean operations at Virginia Mason Medical Center (VMMC) in Seattle, Washington. Soon I was "knee deep" in healthcare consulting thanks to the healthcare president on that historic flight, Mike Rona, and his perceptive and visionary boss,

Lean production: "Lean production," based on the Toyota Production System, is a term applied to the production methods pioneered in Japan after World War II by Kiichiro Toyoda and Taiichi Ohno of the Toyota Motor Corporation. Lean is a production strategy in which all parts of the production system are focused to eliminate waste while continuously increasing the percentage of value-added work. The term was coined by John Krafcik of the International Motor Vehicle Program at Massachusetts Institute of Technology. It was first publicized in the book *The Machine that Changed the World: The Story of Lean Production* by James P. Womack, Daniel T. Jones, and Daniel Roos (1991).

Virginia Mason's chief executive officer (CEO), Dr. Gary Kaplan.

What has my experience shown me? First, healthcare organizations are indeed resistant to change, but no more so than many other organizations (especially if the CEO commits to the change). For example, surgeons are no more (or less) resistant to change than aerospace engineers. Second, Lean thinking (cutting waste by half over and over again) is applicable to any organization—and can pay off big for the healthcare industry in particular.

DRAMATIC IMPROVEMENTS IN HEALTHCARE ARE POSSIBLE!

I'm writing this book for you, the healthcare leader. I'm writing it because our healthcare system needs an overhaul and because I know you would like to improve your own operations—increase patient and staff satisfaction; cut waste, clutter, and confusion; eliminate defects (errors); lower costs; raise profitability; and more.

My main message to you is that dramatic improvements in healthcare are not only possible, but inevitable—if you commit to change and diligently apply Lean thinking, principles, and tools. The real-life examples and case studies in these pages will demonstrate that. To pique your interest, here are some of the benefits the Virginia Mason Hyperbaric Clinic has gained since starting its "model line" (Lean implementation in one part of an organization) in 2005 (Kaplan and Rona 2006):

- Staff workday length has shortened from up to 14 hours to 8 hours, a 42 percent reduction. A second shift is no longer needed.
- Number of patients per attendant in the hyperbaric chambers has increased from an average of 2.4 in the old facility to 5.4 in the new one.
- Treatment hours are up 18 percent.
- Patient wait times have basically disappeared.
- Emergencies are treated simultaneously with routine treatments.
- Ergonomic complaints have been eliminated.
- Transportation by ambulance from the main hospital to the previous facility across the street was eliminated, saving $50,000 a year.
- Margins per patient are up 308 percent.

You'll learn more about this remarkable success story in Chapter 10, but I'll bet you'd like to achieve results like these in your organization. This book is dedicated to helping you do it.

NOT FOR THE FAINT OF HEART

I must advise you from the start, however, that the journey to becoming a world-class healthcare organization isn't quick or easy, or for the impatient or faint of heart. As I have always told my clients, "If you are going uphill and taking one step at a time, you are headed in the right direction." This is not to say that you cannot achieve some quick results within parts of your organization. It's only to point out that implementing large-scale, synchronistic change within the entire organization takes time because, although you may not realize it, you're deep in *muda* (a word the Japanese use to describe waste, meaning any activity, service, or supply that consumes time, money, and other resources, but creates no value).

> *Muda:* Waste, meaning any activity, service, or supply that consumes time, money, and other resources, but creates no value

Toyota has been engaged in its change effort for decades and hasn't run short of improvement ideas yet. The relentless pursuit

Kaizen: Continuous incremental improvement

of continuous incremental improvement is called *kaizen* in Japanese, and it is essential not only to achieving world-class operational performance, but to staying ahead of the competition as well.

PEOPLE ARE KEY

Another important thing to keep in mind is that while technology may sometimes play an important role, the key to success will be your *people*. Organizations often leverage this resource least effectively. The principles I've outlined above are aimed at gaining the greatest possibile return from the skills and ideas of the people who do the work. They are the experts who can identify improvement opportunities and they comprise the creative powerhouse necessary for success. So if you think your organization can achieve the kind of results I've indicated by sitting back and hoping consultants will lead and do the work, think again. Both you and your people must be committed and deeply involved—especially you, the healthcare leader.

Perhaps you're still asking yourself, "How can a manufacturing model apply to healthcare? Patients aren't products put together on an assembly line." That's certainly true and is a perspective you should never forget. Indeed, patients aren't the products—they're the *customers*. Speaking broadly, there's just one product you're trying to provide—*high-quality, defect-free healthcare*. Fortunately, healthcare is susceptible to the same improvement methods as other products or services—providing healthcare is no different, as you will learn, from building cars or airplanes.

THREE GREAT REASONS TO IMPROVE

If becoming a world-class organization isn't enough of a stimulus to get you to embrace Lean, then let me offer three more reasons:

1. *Patients deserve better.* At present, most healthcare delivery is plagued by excessive waiting and other non–value-added time spent by, and paid for by, patients (or their insurers). The patient should only pay for *value-added* activities and time rather than receiving a bill for services that contain as much as *95 percent* non–value-added activities or time. Offering patients an efficient, smooth-flowing, defect-free, and hassle-free experience respectful of their time means greater patient satisfaction and a competitive advantage in the healthcare marketplace.

   Additionally, delayed care tends to be *poor* care. A longer hospital stay, extra waiting time for diagnosis or treatment, or additional procedure time in surgery, for example, correlates with increased rates of infection and other errors. Reducing wasted time, a key Lean strategy, also means reducing the number of handoffs when mistakes are more likely to occur.

2. *Employees deserve better.* There's a direct correlation between high employee satisfaction/morale and productivity. Healthcare employees who work in environments with high percentages of non–value-added activity or idle time grow frustrated, stressed, and angry, especially when they feel the system is broken and not being fixed. Happy workers are much more likely to provide high levels of patient satisfaction than unhappy ones. The employees at Toyota are satisfied, enthusiastic, and highly motivated because they work in a system that rewards problem solving and continuous improvement. Can we say the same about the average healthcare worker?

3. *Our nation deserves better.* The cost of healthcare in the United States is becoming increasingly unaffordable for a growing number of citizens, and is rendering American businesses less competitive in the global marketplace. Unfortunately, the cost is projected to reach 20 percent of the entire U.S. economy by 2014 (National Coalition on Health Care 2007). Economists say increases like this are not sustainable. However, if the healthcare industry as a whole were to adopt proven concepts of Lean operations to reduce wasted

patient and staff time, as well as other resources, thereby creating new capacity, it could spread costs over greater patient volumes and reduce per-patient costs.

But this book isn't about helping you improve the entire U.S. healthcare system. It's about helping you improve your own organization. Hopefully, the kinds of improvements I've indicated that are available through Lean are ones you'd like to achieve. You're probably wondering exactly what implementing Lean entails. What are the elements? How does one apply them?

THREE ESSENTIALS FOR SUCCESS

That's what the rest of the book is about. You can think of the book as a tutorial on applying these methods to your operations. However, I need to stress three things at this point:

1. You have to commit to personally lead the charge and the change (otherwise it won't happen).
2. A master *sensei* (Japanese for a personal trainer with the mastery of a body of knowledge, in this case Lean production) is almost essential to guide you through the improvement process (your typical American-oriented consulting process wrapped around organizational development or Six Sigma principles will not work).

> *Sensei:* Personal trainer with the mastery of a body of knowledge, in this case Lean production

3. You must be willing to commit to a long-term "slog" through the swamp of waste and defects that lies hidden beneath the surface of your daily operations.

Without an understanding that real change is hard and takes time and commitment, your improvement effort will not survive the first year.

LEAN PRODUCTION

Now, let me briefly explain what I mean by Lean Production, or simply Lean, which is based upon the Toyota Production System.

Lean basically focuses on driving waste from the system. You'll learn more in Chapter 2 about the seven kinds of waste, but two obvious ones are *waste of time* and *waste of inventory*. What Lean continually asks is whether a product or service is *value-added*. If not, it is waste. One of Lean's goals is to reduce by half such costs as time spent performing a task, space requirements, and investment in tools—and then repeat this again and again. Gains may become smaller and smaller, but the organization gets closer and closer to *world class*, which we will define as *waste free*.

Although Lean has many elements, its two main pillars are:

1. Just-in-time production: consistently delivering only the healthcare service that is needed, in just the required amount, where it is needed, and when it is needed.
2. *Jidoka*: the intelligent use of both people and technology, with the ability (even obligation) to stop any process at the first sign of an abnormality; in other words, a system that keeps the patient safe, not that gets them harmed or killed.

THE SEVEN HEALTHCARE FLOWS

You'll learn more about the application of these principles to healthcare as we proceed through the book. You'll also see how they relate to the seven flows in a healthcare environment. The seven flows are:

1. Flow of patients,
2. Flow of clinicians,
3. Flow of medication,
4. Flow of supplies,

5. Flow of information,
6. Flow of equipment, and
7. Flow of process engineering.

These flows are described in detail in Chapter 7. Suffice it to say for now that *flow* is a very important concept in Lean production. "Toyota's system is primarily about flow—information flow, physical flow of parts, overall production flow—via standardized processes and continuous improvement" (Bohmer and Ferlins 2006). The idea is to eliminate delays and obstacles along the line of production or, in the case of healthcare, in delivering a service.

Efficient flow minimizes *lead time*, or the total time a customer (patient) must wait to receive a product (or service) after placing an order (requesting a service). The more lead time is compressed, the more efficient the use of resources and the more satisfied the customer. As you'll see later, one way to reduce lead time is for the patient to "pull" himself through the system (go at his own pace without being "pushed" by staff, known as "pull production"). Through the application of Lean, Virginia Mason was able to reduce overall patient lead time by 53 percent, or the equivalent of 708 days of patient time (Bohmer and Ferlins 2006).

Pull production: System where parts, supplies, information, and services are pulled by internal and external customers exactly when they are needed

FACING REAL CHANGE CAN BE INTIMIDATING

If what I've said so far seems both daunting and strange to you, don't worry. Real change usually appears that way. That's why it's often avoided, even when needed.

Remember, though, that knowledgeable people are available to help (see the Afterword) and also that the process proceeds one step at a time. The most critical factor in success is your commitment and personal stewardship of the process as the healthcare leader, because successful, large-scale improvement efforts such as those I've been discussing always occur from the *top down*. The first step is a change in *mind-set*. It's believing that dramatic improvement is possible and that you can lead the change. I have always maintained—as Bill Conway, CEO of Conway Quality, used to tell us at Boeing—that "If you have the will, the belief, and the wherewithal, then you can do it."

If you're still with me, let's get started.

CHAPTER TAKEAWAYS

- Healthcare organizations are no more resistant to change than other organizations.
- Lean thinking (cutting waste by half over and over again) is applicable to any organization.
- Dramatic improvements in healthcare are possible with Lean.
- The journey is not for the impatient or faint of heart. Real change is hard and takes time and commitment.
- The relentless pursuit of continuous incremental improvement (*kaizen*) is essential to achieving world-class operational performance.
- The assistance of a Japanese master *sensei* (teacher) or a consultant trained by a *sensei* is recommended.
- People are your most important resource.

REFERENCES

Bohmer, R.M.J., and E.M. Ferlins. 2006. "Virginia Mason Medical Center." *Harvard Business Review,* September (online revision of article originally published in October 2005). http://harvardbusinessonline.hbsp.harvard.edu.

Kaplan, G.S., and J.M. Rona. 2006. "Seeking Zero Defects ... Applying the Toyota Production System to Health Care—Five Years Later." Presentation to the Institute for Healthcare Improvement, December 10.

National Coalition on Health Care. 2007. "Facts on the Cost of Health Care" [Online white paper; retrieved 10/25/07.] www.nchc.org/facts/2007%20updates/cost.pdf.

Womack, J.P., D.T. Jones., and D. Roos. 1991. *The Machine that Changed the World: The Story of Lean Production,* reprint edition, New York: Harper Perennial.

CHAPTER 2

Eliminating Waste Will Transform American Healthcare

OVERVIEW: In this chapter, "waste" is defined as any expenditure of time, money, or other resources that does not add value, that is, contribute to the efficient delivery of healthcare to the patient. The most extreme example of waste is poor care, resulting in death or injury to the patient. Another example is soaring healthcare costs. As in manufacturing, there are seven kinds of waste in healthcare. Examples of each are provided. The Lean expert's job is to find the waste and eliminate it quickly. This requires the efficient use of the healthcare system's most important resource—its people.

Lean operations give us a new understanding of waste. With this new understanding, we find waste in all the ways work is done. With the principles and processes of Lean, we know how to reduce and eliminate waste, including the reduction and elimination of errors (defects).

First of all, Lean operations begin with a definition of purpose. For healthcare, state the purpose in terms of the patient, perhaps something like this:

Our purpose is health maintenance and the successful diagnosis and treatment of patient illness. The patient is the customer of the healthcare system. The patient comes first.

With this focus, waste in the healthcare system is any expenditure of time or resources that does not contribute to the efficient delivery of quality healthcare to the patient. In the typical medical center today, waste is found in the traditional structure, policies, and practices of daily operations. I would stress that it does not result from a lack of education, ability, or commitment on the part of healthcare professionals. They are usually part of an operational structure that produces waste. In this chapter, you'll see how.

THE EFFECTS OF WASTE

Patients at Risk

Tragically, hospital mistakes cause a significant number of deaths in the United States. Based on two seminal hospital studies involving data from three U.S. states, the proportion of hospital admissions experiencing an adverse event—injury or death—is between 2.9 percent and 3.7 percent. Even taking the lower figure, *hospital safety is 97.1 percent perfect at best.* Or, viewed the other way around, there's at least a 2.9 percent chance that a preventable adverse event will affect someone who is hospitalized. In fact, "the results of these two studies imply that at least 44,000 and perhaps as many as 98,000 Americans die in hospitals each year as a result of medical errors" (Kohn, Corrigan, and Donaldson 2000).

Hospital errors, according to a report by the Institute of Medicine, kill more Americans than breast cancer, traffic accidents, or AIDS. The report estimated the annual national costs of preventable adverse healthcare events to be between $8.5 billion and $14.5 billion (Kohn, Corrigan, and Donaldson 2000). Yet, in a survey of 831 physicians in April to July of 2002 by the Harvard School of Public Health and the Kaiser Family Foundation, *only*

5 percent of physicians (and 6 percent of the public) said medical errors were a top healthcare concern (Blendon et al. 2002).

However, preventable deaths, tragic as they are, are only one symptom of a U.S. healthcare system that is broken.

Rising Costs, Declining Coverage, Falling Satisfaction

We Americans are often told we have the best healthcare system in the world. We certainly have *the most expensive* healthcare system in the world, one estimated to have cost us *$2.2 trillion* in 2006, or $7,129 per person. And the costs keep climbing. In 2004, the United States spent 16 percent of its gross national product on healthcare, and the cost is projected to reach 20 percent by 2014 if present trends continue (National Coalition on Health Care 2007).

For many people and businesses, the cost is reaching a breaking point. According to a 2006 Kaiser Family Foundation study, the average annual premiums for employer-sponsored healthcare plans in 2006 were $4,242 for single coverage and $11,480 for family coverage. Of these amounts, employees paid an average of 16 percent for single coverage and 27 percent for family coverage. However, employee premiums are going up—87 percent since 2000 for family coverage. And in 2008, the average *Fortune* 500 company may spend more on healthcare than it makes in profit (Kaiser Family Foundation and Health Research and Educational Trust 2006).

Even so, nearly 47 million Americans lack health insurance—more than 40 percent of people under age 65. With or without it, people file for bankruptcy at a rate of one every 30 seconds because of medical bills (Barry and Basler 2007).

In spite of the enormous cost, the U.S. healthcare system is not producing outcomes consistent with the outlay of dollars. Perhaps most telling is a 2006 poll by *USA Today*, ABC News, and the Kaiser Family Foundation showing that only 44 percent of Americans said they were satisfied with the quality of healthcare in the United States (Appleby 2006).

But at least those who can afford it get the best healthcare in the world, right? Not exactly.

Lagging Behind Other Countries

"Many countries around the world take far better care of their people and achieve better results from their healthcare systems, and do it all with fewer dollars," say investigative journalists Donald L. Bartlett and James B. Steele in their carefully documented book *Critical Condition: How Health Care in America Became Big Business and Bad Medicine* (2004).

As they point out in a sobering World Health Organization global ranking of healthcare based on access to healthcare and the fairness of financing, the United States came in a distant 37th place, between Costa Rica and Slovenia.

CAUSES OF HEALTHCARE WASTE

The loss of life and injuries from errors are tragic examples of waste in the U.S. healthcare system, but waste is everywhere. And, again, let's be clear—the waste is not the fault of the individuals in our system, but the *system itself*, which is overly complex, rife with outdated procedures, and redundant. For example, a 1993 study of nurses at a hospital in Hillsdale, Illinois, found the staff spent only 40 percent of their time on patient care; the rest was consumed by "communication, coordination, hotel services, documentation, transportation, and administrative issues" (Lee, Clarke, and Glassford 1993). A 2000 study at the University of Pittsburgh Medical Center concluded that "the staff was spending more time nursing the system than nursing patients" (Thompson, Wolfe, and Spear 2003).

According to the National Coalition on Health Care, "Experts agree that our healthcare system is riddled with inefficiencies;

excessive administrative expenses; inflated prices; poor management; and inappropriate care, waste, and fraud" (National Coalition on Health Care 2007). Richard Dayo, professor of medicine at the University of Washington in Seattle, says, "Several credible estimates have come up with around 30 percent of healthcare is unnecessary" (Appleby 2006).

One of the main challenges to the healthcare industry is the *inefficiency of the traditional hospital structure*. For example, hospital layouts frequently force patients and staff to travel long distances onsite, encountering many delays. Hospital employees also spend countless hours processing and distributing paperwork, and the work is so fragmented that usually no one is fully aware of all aspects of the patient's status.

In my experience in the healthcare arena, more than 90 percent of the time required to provide services is *non–value-added* and mainly results from the healthcare system's traditional centralized structure (some of the non–value-added activity is required by government regulation). For example, in a personal study of time my wife spent receiving ultrasound treatment in the hospital, only 35 minutes of the two hours she was there were spent actually receiving treatment. That amounts to less than 30 percent value-added time (Black 1998).

THE SEVEN WASTES IN THE HEALTHCARE SYSTEM

Waste in the healthcare system is no different from waste in manufacturing systems. That's why we can provide healthcare examples for the seven categories of waste that Taiichi Ohno, author of *Toyota Production System: Beyond Large-Scale Production* (1988), identified in manufacturing systems (Figure 2.1). It's also why Lean can provide the solution in healthcare as well as in manufacturing.

Figure 2.1 Taiichi Ohno's Seven Wastes

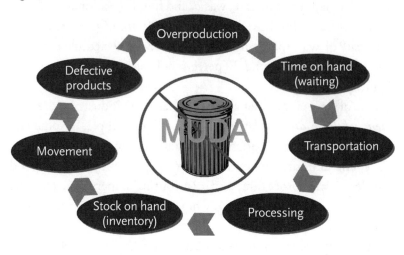

Waste of Overproduction

In some cases, redundancy is prudent, as in having backup supplies of lifesaving medications. In most cases, it is sheer waste and represents a failure to understand what is really needed.

Waste of Overproduction:
- Making photocopies of a form that is never used
- Providing copies of reports to people who have not asked for them and will not actually read them
- Processing piles of documents that sit in queue at the next workstation
- CCing e-mail unnecessarily

At Park Nicollet Health Services (PNHS) in Minneapolis, all lab results were printed at the main lab in one big batch, sorted by location, mailed to various clinics, sorted by department name, mailed to the department, sorted by clinician name, and finally delivered to the clinician. This process could take days. Now lab results are printed directly to individual departments at each clinic multiple times a day and distributed directly to the clinician.

At Virginia Mason Medical Center (VMMC), the standard practice was to ask patients the same questions at each stop along the "value stream" (the specific activities required to provide a specific service to the patient). This resulted in repetition and rework, and was exasperating to the patients because they had to repeat their answers over and over. By implementing an online-documentation system, the information is now contained on one form that follows the patient. It only needs to be completed once and the patient is asked questions only once.

Waste of Time on Hand (Waiting)

Time is critical in healthcare settings. In some cases, it can make the difference between life and death. But for most patients, time is often spent in long queues, or waiting at the wrong place, or walking too far for a meeting or a procedure.

At the Virginia Mason Emergency Department, the average wait time for a patient to be seen by a care provider was 20 minutes. After an improvement in the process based on Lean principles, the wait time was reduced to six minutes.

At Park Nicollet, applying standard work (a prescribed, repeatable sequence of steps) to patient set-up helped reduce day-of-service lead time (the time required to complete a patient event) from two hours to nine minutes.

Waste of Stock on Hand (Inventory)

Inventory builds up in healthcare systems and, if not culled on a regular basis, can become obsolete and require disposal. This is

> **Value stream:** The specific activities required to provide a specific service to the patient

> **Waste of Time on Hand (Waiting)**
> - Patients waiting to see their physician
> - Clinic service representatives waiting on the phone to schedule appointments
> - Early morning admissions waiting for surgeries that won't be performed until later in the day
> - Patients waiting for support services such as internal transport
> - Staff waiting for office equipment (e.g., computer or photocopier) to be repaired before being able to do work
> - Staff waiting for a meeting that is starting late

> **Standard work:** A prescribed, repeatable sequence of steps (or actions) that balances people's work to *takt* time

costly, requires space and energy to store, and requires time and energy to move.

Waste of Stock on Hand (Inventory)
- Stockpiling office and clinical supplies that won't be used for weeks or months
- Storing excess supplies whose "use by" date expires before they're used
- Maintaining expensive implants that can be ordered on a just-in-time basis

Kanban: A way of automatically signaling when new parts, supplies, or services are needed. In Japanese, *kanban* means sign, signboard, doorplate, poster, billboard, or card, but is taken more broadly to mean any kind of signal.

Rapid Process Improvement Workshop (RPIW or *kaizen* event): A team of people who do the work, fully engaged in a rigorous and disciplined five-day process, using the tools of Lean to achieve immediate results in the elimination of waste

At Park Nicollet, inventory of medications ranks third on the expense list; therefore, managing this inventory is crucial to the financial health of the organization. In three departments at one clinic site, approximately 628 individual containers of medication were stored with an overall price tag of $32,513. Of this amount, 28 percent were high-cost, low-use medications—items regularly stocked but infrequently used. Through the implementation of *kanban* (a way of automatically signaling when new parts, supplies, or services are needed) to control the stock on hand, improvement teams eliminated 29 percent of the stock in one location and reduced cost by 50 percent.

At Virginia Mason, a great deal of movement and inventory were wasted as nursing supplies were moved from a supply closet down the hall to the bedside. An improvement team worked with the engineering department to design and build clear plastic containers that hang on the wall and hold supplies at point of use, close to the patient. Supply inventory already has been significantly reduced. The target is to reduce inventory by 90 percent every time a Rapid Process Improvement Workshop (RPIW) is conducted.

Waste of Movement

It's common for more than 70 percent of a healthcare facility's budget to be allocated to salaries and wages. Therefore, optimal use of staff time is essential to profitability. It's also respectful of employees' time.

At Park Nicollet, one of the radiology technologists was walking up to five miles a day moving equipment to where it was needed. The radiology department is now working on minimizing this waste of time and movement by placing the equipment at point of use, or at least closer to the technician.

Virginia Mason reduced the amount of "walk time" (time spent walking from one location to another) by locating registered nurses (RNs) and patient care technicians (PCTs) in a common "cell" (work area) on the nursing floors. This improvement reduced the number of steps a nurse travels during a work shift from 5,818 steps to 846, an 85.5 percent reduction. It reduced PCT steps from 2,664 steps to 1,258, a 53 percent reduction.

Waste of Movement
- Physicians and staff looking for items that should be clearly labeled
- Physicians walking to another location to check an online note during a patient exam
- Clinicians going from one building on campus to another to attend a meeting

Walk time: Time spent walking from one location to another

Cell: Work area

Waste of Defective Products (Generically, Defects)

In healthcare facilities, defects often show up as errors in charted or recorded information. These types of defects can have a severe negative impact on the quality of patient care. Many medical centers are taking stringent action to make defect reduction and mistake proofing key components of their patient-care strategy.

Early in its Lean implementation, Virginia Mason put in place a system whereby any staff member can stop any process or procedure ("stop the line") if he believes proceeding would adversely affect patient safety. These interventions are called "patient safety alerts" (PSAs). As of the end of 2006, staff had stopped the line 4,753 times, with the major categories of concern being systems issues (39

Waste of Defective Products (Defects)

- Fixing errors made in documents
- Misfiling documents
- Dealing with service complaints
- Making mistakes due to incorrect information or miscommunication
- Filling out inpatient admission cards incorrectly
- Handwriting orders in an illegible manner
- Sending bills with an incorrect address

Andon: Visual control device, usually a light, that alerts supervisors to factory floor needs or problems

Waste in Transportation

- Moving individual files from one location to another
- Moving supplies into and out of a storage area
- Moving equipment for surgeries in and out of the operating room
- Moving equipment for procedures in and out of procedure rooms
- Transferring charts from other buildings onsite

percent), diagnosis and treatment issues (25 percent), and medication errors (20 percent).

Park Nicollet focused on creating a patient tracking system (PTS) to reduce defects. All patients scheduled to have surgery must have completed a series of activities before the surgery. Examples of these activities include providing a completed medical history, completing a physical, signing consent forms, and having patients' special needs met (e.g., providing an interpreter).

As patients are scheduled for surgery, they're entered into the PTS. As a patient completes each preparatory step, her progress is tracked with a light-indicator system (*andon* or visual control device). A green light indicates all items have been met and the patient is a "go" for surgery. A yellow light indicates that one or more of the items needs resolution. If any items have not been completed 24 hours prior to the surgery, the yellow light turns red, indicating that action must be completed immediately to ensure readiness for surgery. Each patient is assigned a preoperative information coordinator who ensures all items are on track, thereby reducing the chance of a surgery cancellation.

Waste in Transportation

Transporting and moving people, equipment, and supplies also burns the time and energy of staff and the system. Reducing movement time can result in tremendous cost containment and better use of staff knowledge and resources.

Park Nicollet owns 22 vans that deliver information, mail, patient files, films, packages, etc., throughout the entire Park Nicollet system. These vans drive more than 342,000 miles per year (equivalent to driving 14 times around the earth). One way PNHS has reduced the miles traveled is by upgrading to an electronic medical record system for handling charts and radiology reports, decreasing the number of files and films to transport by van.

In the Virginia Mason Neurology Clinic, patient charts were automatically ordered prior to each patient visit. These were being transported to and from medical records, which is located two blocks from the clinic. After careful observation it was determined that often the charts were neither used nor needed. The neurology team decided to stop delivery of all charts, except the few that were actually needed, saving a great deal of unnecessary transportation and handling.

Waste in Processing

The waste embedded in processing takes the form of rework, multiple duplications of material, and hard-copy versus electronic-copy inputs and outputs.

At Virginia Mason, after careful observation it was determined that only those patients suffering back pain who were surgical candidates needed a magnetic resonance image (MRI) to assist the surgeon. Eliminating MRIs for non-surgical back-pain patients saved both time and money—about $3,000 for each eliminated MRI, including pre- and post-treatment.

All patients in Park Nicollet's Eating Disorders Institute (EDI) go through an initial assessment process to determine if they're good candidates for EDI's services, and, if so, where in EDI they should start (inpatient, partial

> **Waste in Processing**
> - Performing tests that aren't needed
> - Redundant capture of information on admission
> - Recording and logging of the same data multiple times
> - Writing information by hand, when direct input to a word processor could eliminate this step
> - Producing a paper copy when a computer file is sufficient

inpatient, intensive outpatient, or outpatient). Before the application of Lean, a patient assessment involved several different types of care providers for each patient, even if one of them determined early on that a patient wasn't a good candidate for EDI. After Lean improvements, the assessments begin with the psychologist. Patients are not sent on for further assessment by the other potential providers unless the psychologist believes they are good candidates for EDI services.

THE JOB OF THE LEAN EXPERT: FIND THE WASTE

Waste can be found in almost every work environment, and time and resources are often required to detect it. It's the job of the Lean expert to analyze a work environment and identify all the opportunities for improvement. He must be able to observe from above and see how the entire system flows. At other times, he must be able to analyze with the microscopic vision of the neurosurgeon and be able to dissect the bits and pieces of a process flow.

Careful observation and reliable documentation can help identify both the waste in an area and opportunities for improvement. Once waste is eliminated, people within the system are often surprised to realize how disruptive the waste was and how they'd simply learned to live with it.

YOUR MOST VALUABLE RESOURCE: PEOPLE

The biggest waste in industry, including healthcare, is hard to see: the failure to leverage resources. History tells us repeatedly that the most powerful resource available to companies is not technology, but people. Focusing on people and empowering them to use their potential is the key to world-class competitiveness. A strong team of people from all levels of the organization, using Lean principles, can help eliminate waste. And by involving everyone in *kaizen* (continuous incremental improvement), Lean also can improve team spirit and morale.

Motivating and engaging your employees is the task of leadership, a subject we'll discuss in Chapter 6, "Building *Kaizen* Leaders." Before we go into detail about how Lean is being applied to healthcare, however, let's look at where Lean thinking comes from.

CHAPTER TAKEAWAYS

- The heart of Lean is eliminating waste. In the healthcare system, waste is any expenditure of time or resources that does not contribute to the efficient delivery of quality healthcare to the patient.
- Death or injury because of poor healthcare is the worst kind of waste in the healthcare industry.
- There are seven types of waste in the healthcare system: overproduction, waste of time, too much inventory, wasted movement, defects, waste in transporting items, and waste in processing.
- The healthcare system itself creates most of the waste.

REFERENCES

Appleby, J. 2006. "Consumer Unease with U.S. Healthcare Grows." *USA Today* October 16, 1A and 4A.

Barry, P., and B. Basler. 2007. "Healing Our System." *AARP Bulletin* March, 12–14.

Bartlett, D.L., and J.B. Steele. 2004. *Critical Condition: How Health Care in America Became Big Business and Bad Medicine.* New York: Doubleday.

Black, J.R. 1998. *A World Class Production System.* Menlo Park, CA: Crisp Publications.

Blendon, J., C.M. DesRoches, M. Brodie, J.M. Benson, A.B. Rosen, E. Schneider, D.E. Altman, K. Zapert, M.J. Herrmann, and A.E. Steffenson. 2002. "Views of Practicing Physicians and the Public on Medical Errors." *New England Journal of Medicine* 347 (24): 1933–40.

Kaiser Family Foundation and Health Research and Educational Trust. 2006. *Employer Health Benefits.* [Online white paper; retrieved 11/1/2007.] www.kff.org/insurance/7527/upload/7527.pdf

Kohn, L.T., J.M. Corrigan, and M.S. Donaldson, eds. 2000. *To Err Is Human: Building a Safer Health System.* Washington, D.C.: National Academies Press.

Lee, J.G., R.W. Clarke, and G.H. Glassford. 1993. "Physicians Can Benefit from a Patient-Focused Hospital." *Physician Executive* 19 (1): 36–38.

National Coalition on Health Care. 2007. "Facts on the Cost of Health Care." [Online white paper; retrieved 10/25/07.] www.nchc.org/facts/2007%20updates/cost.pdf.

Ohno, T. 1988. *Toyota Production System: Beyond Large-Scale Production.* New York: Productivity Press.

Thompson, D.N., G.A. Wolf, and S.J. Spear. 2003. "Driving Improvement in Patient Care: Lessons from Toyota." *Journal of Nursing Administration* 33 (11): 585–95.

CHAPTER 3

A Brief History of Lean

OVERVIEW: Elements of Lean thinking go back hundreds of years, but as a system of production and management, Lean is the product of three seminal thinkers from Japan: Sakichi Toyoda; his son, Kiichiro; and Taiichi Ohno, Toyota Motor Company's former chief process engineer. Together they created the Toyota Production System, which provided the basis for the further development of Lean principles. The author's experience with Lean was at Boeing, where it eventually replaced most other quality programs and is still defined as the Boeing Production System. Lean experts from Japan—*senseis*, or master trainers—played a critical role. A chance meeting on an airplane led the author to become the first to fully apply Lean to healthcare using Japanese methods.

EARLY BEGINNINGS

The Lean approach to production is not new—in fact, one could argue that Lean existed in crude form quite a while back. In the late 1500s, the Republic of Venice relied on rapid production techniques to survive. The Venice arsenal—mostly comprised of galleys (warships)—

was produced by the largest industrial plant in the world at that time and the world's first large-scale assembly line (Swartz 1994).

The plant employed 1,500 workers and covered 60 acres. Supervisors ensured that all components were made in compliance with established standards, which allowed the components to be used on any Venetian galley. Standard operations similar to Toyota's were in place throughout the galley assembly line.

More than two centuries later, weapons again were the focus of improved operations. While in France, Thomas Jefferson saw how the French used standardized parts in the manufacture of firearms. As vice president, Jefferson persuaded the U.S. military to require interchangeability of parts in a 1798 contract for 10,000 muskets.

Eli Whitney accepted the challenge and built a factory in New Haven, Connecticut. Many advanced production techniques were applied to production, including the use of ordered and integrated workflow; standardized, interchangeable parts; focused factory areas; dedicated machines; and even error-proofing mechanisms to reduce variations introduced by personal handwork.

Still later, Henry Ford led a revolution of a different kind. The secret to Ford's success was a new process model for automobile manufacturing—continuous-flow assembly. Between 1913 and 1914, Ford doubled production with no increase in the workforce. Between 1920 and 1926, cycle time was reduced by 90 percent—from 21 days to 2 days (Swartz 1994).

THE TOYOTA PRODUCTION SYSTEM

Sakichi Toyoda, who founded the Toyota Group, was the inventor of a loom that would stop automatically if any of the threads snapped. His invention reduced defects and raised yields, since a loom would not continue producing imperfect fabric and using up thread after a problem occurred. The new loom also enabled a single operator to handle dozens of looms, revolutionizing the textile industry.

The principle of designing equipment to stop automatically and call attention to problems immediately is crucial to the Toyota Production System (TPS). This is the system of *jidoka* discussed in more detail in later chapters. It is evident on every production line at Toyota and at other companies that use the same system.

When the Toyota Group set up an automobile-manufacturing operation in the 1930s (replacing the Toyoda family's "d" with a "t"), Sakichi's son Kiichiro headed the new venture. He traveled to the United States to study Henry Ford's system in operation. He then returned to Japan with a strong grasp of Ford's conveyor system and an even stronger desire to adapt that system to the small volumes of the Japanese market (Public Affairs Division of Toyota 1988).

> *Jidoka*: The intelligent use of both people and technology, with the ability (even obligation) to stop any process at the first sign of an abnormality. In other words, a system that keeps the patient safe, not that gets them harmed or killed.

Soon thereafter, the first Toyota system of manufacturing was born. To say that Toyota copied Ford is not accurate—Toyota learned from Ford, especially from Ford's mistakes. This demonstrates the driving power of the Toyota system: continuous improvement.

The Toyota system was in some ways a revolution, just as Ford's had been. The differences between how Toyota and Ford built cars were often striking. One difference was that Ford relied on maximum lot sizes and minimum numbers of setups. Toyota, on the other hand, strove to reduce lot sizes to eventually produce each and every product uniquely.

Another big difference was in the control of production. *Kanban* (a way of signaling when new parts or supplies are needed) was used as the major tool in Toyota's "just-in-time" production. For example, "when assembly-line workers begin to use parts from bins (hinges, door handles, windshield wipers), they take out a *kanban* card and put it in a mailbox. A material handler will come and pick it up and go back to a store to replenish what is used on the assembly line" (Liker 2004).

A third key difference was in the arrangement of equipment. Instead of grouping all machines together by type of machine—all of the lathes here, all of the milling machines over there, for example—Toyota arranged the machines in the order they were used in the manufacturing process. This enabled low inventories and small lot sizes. All these changes were revolutionary to automobile manufacturing.

Taiichi Ohno, Toyota's chief process engineer, who added many of the tools and detailed production processes to Kiichiro Toyoda's vision, understood that what would soon become TPS could be applied more broadly than just to manufacturing. In his book *Toyota Production System: Beyond Large-Scale Production* (1988), he states:

> The Toyota production system, however, is not just a production system. I am confident it will reveal its strength as a management system adapted to today's era of global markets and high-level computerized information systems.

LEAN COMES TO BOEING

I arrived at Boeing in 1978, at a time when the aerospace industry was on an upward cycle. I brought with me some perspectives I had developed during my service in the U.S. Army—including two tours in Vietnam—where I conducted my own research into waste, in this case waste in war. Upon my arrival at Boeing, I soon discovered that many of the same concepts I was dealing with in the Army applied to the corporate realm. It wasn't long after I started my Boeing career that the company began examining—and attempting to apply—the "total quality" teachings of Dr. W. Edwards Deming and Dr. Joseph Juran that played such an important role in making Japanese industry competitive.

A Special Challenge: Embracing Change When Things Are Going Well

As Boeing began the slow and sometimes painful process of changing its ways, we faced the usual obstacles as well as one we had overlooked—the fact that business was great! We were the number one commercial aircraft manufacturer in the world, with a comfortable lead in market share. The air-travel market was booming and orders were pouring in with no end in sight. We were expanding, looking into the new aircraft program that would eventually become the 777. The future looked bright. There were no crises, or so we thought.

So why worry? Because we knew that success today guarantees absolutely nothing tomorrow. We, meaning those of us beginning to learn about quality-improvement thinking, knew we had many opportunities to improve.

Here's how Bruce Gissing, then the executive vice president for operations for the Boeing Commercial Airplane Group, remembers the general thinking in the company at that time:

> "If it ain't broke, don't fix it" was an underlying theme. We had gone through market cycles, but always came out of them bruised but not hurt. The "method of choice" for contending with the cycle was massive layoffs. The Boeing psyche when a consultant suggested that we could improve our operations was skepticism. Our retort was always "we are different"—simply put, we were arrogant.
>
> The "case for change" was nonexistent. Yes, there were people like John Black agitating, but they were ignored. Occasionally, the leadership would launch a program like Quality Circles, Zero Defects, etc., but they fizzled after a short, frenzied life. (Gissing 2004)

First Steps

The quality effort at Boeing—under the designation of "continuous quality improvement" (CQI)—was started by Bill Selby, director of operations for defense and space, when I began reporting to him in early 1983. Selby and I were pioneers at Boeing. We were the first at Boeing to start Quality of Work Life programs as part of productivity improvement.

We benchmarked several leading corporations, drafted the first company quality plan, and established the company's first quality center in 1984. In the spring of 1985, Boeing Aerospace Company (BAC) president Bud Hebeler invited Dr. Juran to present his seminar "Upper Management and Quality" to BAC executives.

The president hosted Dr. Juran at a private dinner. There, Selby asked Dr. Juran to estimate the cost of poor quality at BAC. Without hesitating, Juran responded "30 percent of sales." This was a huge number. There was silence as the meal continued.

Boeing's quality-improvement journey was soon launched with the formation of 12 Quality Councils led by senior executives. This was followed by quality training for more than 85,000 employees, including more than 8,000 managers and 43,000 hourly employees. We also targeted all other payrolls (general office, technical, engineering, and administration) in what became one of the industry's major change-management efforts.

Cementing Quality Improvement as a "Way of Life": Japan Study Missions

In the years leading up to 1990, we increasingly moved toward "total quality." But I wasn't convinced that we had really found our one, true, companywide path to becoming a "world-class company"—and I was concerned that Boeing leadership hadn't really decided to fully embrace quality improvement as the Boeing "way of life."

Boeing leaders were making speeches about our 60 percent market share, our number one position in the world, and the fact that rival Airbus could never catch us. When I looked at our performance metrics, however, I concluded they were mediocre. I believed that to move Boeing to the next level of performance we needed to go to Japan to study world-class companies and then create a new vision for Boeing.

I was now reporting to Bruce Gissing, the executive vice president for Operations for the Boeing Commercial Airplane Group, who had been assigned to that position in January of 1990. The toughest job I had was getting Bruce to commit to take a team to Japan and study "world class." I walked the halls of Boeing telling whoever would listen to me that just because we had 60 percent market share for commercial airliners didn't mean we had world-class metrics. It was a tough sell.

In early 1990, we, a team of Boeing executives led by Gissing and involved in leading the quality effort, embarked on our first study mission to Japan. This trip would not have happened without Bruce Gissing's insistence that we had to go. Preparation for the trip included 45 hours of classroom training and required reading five books about the Japanese revolution. The trip itself lasted two weeks. We visited eight companies all well into their quality journeys, including the Union of Japanese Scientists and Engineers and, of course, Toyota.

At the end of the mission, we took a final written essay examination at the Imperial Hotel in Tokyo encompassing 27 questions. To put it mildly, participants' eyes were opened. As one manager commented: "Thank God Toyota is not in the aerospace industry."

After our return to the States, Gissing put us on a rigid schedule to implement our action plans from Japan. We met every month through November of 1990. The formation of the BCAG Strategy Council in February 1991 set the stage for a major full-court press focused on world-class competitiveness principles learned in Japan.

Our team was followed by six more teams through the end of 1991, a total of 99 executives that included chairman and CEO Frank Shrontz and all of Boeing's presidents, general managers, and other executives, down to the director level. These visits taught us that the basis of competitive success was shifting *away* from technology as a competitive advantage toward *greater efficiency* at manufacturing and process development by applying total quality control as the *management* system. This observation played a crucial role in focusing efforts at Boeing on creating competitive advantage.

Over the Hump

We were finally "over the hump" and had a critical mass of top-level support for our quality efforts. Boeing leaders directed construction of a course called World Class Competitiveness (WCC). The objectives of that course were:

- to create a common language of change and improvement for everyone at Boeing,
- to heighten our sense of urgency as a company, and
- to increase openness to change.

Eventually all Boeing managers, more than 10,000 in all, attended four-day seminars during which they were introduced to successful, world-class Japanese manufacturing methods. They in turn cascaded the training down to the first-line supervisory level. First-line supervisors then trained their employees. The entire workforce—more than 100,000 employees—was then trained in WCC in 24 months, unheard of in a corporation the size of Boeing.

Over 1994 to 1996, defects in production were reduced 35 percent and customer complaints dropped accordingly. Where applied, Lean reduced the typical floor space required for operations by 50 percent and cut the amount of inventory kept on hand by 30 to 70 percent (Boeing Company 1997).

Finding Boeing's *Senseis*

However, in my view, the point at which Boeing became truly committed to WCC principles was the introduction of *senseis* to Boeing with the mission to implement the Toyota Production System. Our Boeing quality-leadership team met with *senseis* Yoshiki Iwata, chairman and CEO of Shingijutsu Global Consulting, and Chihiro Nakao, Shingijutsu's president. Both had previously reported to Taiichi Ohno, father of TPS, in Toyota's *Kaizen* Promotion Office. Signing them to a contract with Boeing was a major coup. Shingijutsu still consults with Boeing today, and the Boeing 737 is being built on a moving production line replicated from Toyota's factories.

The latter is one of the breakthrough successes of applying Lean to Boeing. Here's how one writer described this process in *Airways* magazine:

> Perhaps the most radical change was to move production from a static, slanted assembly to a straight line that moves continuously. The "naked fuselage" is trucked into one end of the Renton (Washington) plant when it arrives from Wichita, and, over the next five to six days, has wiring assemblies and interior systems installed. An additional day is then needed for the wings and, most importantly, the landing gear to be attached. From that moment … it will move down the line on its own wheels. It is a remarkable sight to see an airplane, starting with a fuselage bereft of tail, wings, engine, or nose cone, ending 700 feet (210 m) later as a fully outfitted Boeing 737 ready to fly. The production line moves at a constant rate of two inches (5 cm) per minute. (Forward 2004)

Only those involved in the aerospace industry may realize what a change this type of production represents, but I can assure you that Lean has made the critical difference in Boeing's current success and perhaps even survival. By 1999, the entire Boeing Company was embracing Lean. Based on TPS, Boeing's system is called the Boeing Production System.

BEYOND BOEING: SOME RESULTS

Boeing wasn't the only company applying Lean principles during this time. Below are validated averages of improvements gained by numerous companies through the application of Lean. Many of them are aerospace related. These results were determined subsequent to a five-year evaluation by the author as Director of Research-World Class Company Studies, The Boeing Company. Companies ranged from one to seven years in Lean principles application and execution.

Direct Labor/Productivity Improved	45–75 percent
Cost Reduced	25–55 percent
Throughput/Flow Increased	60–90 percent
Defects/Scrap Reduced	50–90 percent
Inventory Reduced	60–90 percent
Space Reduced	35–50 percent
Lead Time Reduced	50–90 percent

ON TO HEALTHCARE

I retired from Boeing in 1999 with the intention of offering what I knew about Lean to other companies in other industries. As I said in Chapter 1, because of the healthcare industry's inward focus and "cottage-like" structure, I didn't foresee the healthcare industry being one of them.

This was true even though I viewed the healthcare industry as one where inefficiency reigned, and I felt very strongly that patients deserved better healthcare than they were getting. But let's be honest, when you're offering a product with "inelastic demand" (i.e., people have to have it), complacency not only can set in, but be shielded from the usual competitive pressure to improve efficiency.

So, I wasn't looking for business in healthcare when it came to me on that flight to Atlanta in the fall of 2000. However, as an interesting note, my wife, Joanne Poggetti, who was a protégé of Dr. W. Edwards Deming, had started her own consulting firm while I was still with Boeing. She'd signed a contract with a healthcare system and started them on the road to Lean in 1996. She became the first person to take a group of healthcare CEOs to Japan to attend Shingijutsu's *gemba kaizen* (training that occurs on the factory floor via real-life problem solving) at Hitachi. That was in October of that year.

> **Gemba Kaizen:** Training that occurs on the factory floor via real-life problem solving

CHAPTER TAKEAWAYS

- Lean thinking in its modern form is the product of three seminal thinkers from the Toyota Motor Company.
- The author's initial experience with Lean was at the Boeing Company, where it eventually replaced most other quality programs.
- Japan study missions helped Boeing leaders understand what could be achieved through Lean.
- Lean experts from Japan—*senseis*, or master teachers—also played a critical role in making Lean Boeing's way of doing business.
- A chance meeting with a healthcare executive on a plane led the author to examine the applicability of Lean to healthcare.

REFERENCES

The Boeing Company. 1997. "Boeing/McDonnell Douglas Merger Documentation." April 4.

Forward, D.C. 2004. "Boeing's Lean Production Machine." *Airways* October, p. 25.

Gissing, B. 2004. Unpublished statement, September 13.

Liker, J.K. 2004. *The Toyota Way: 14 Management Principles from the World's Greatest Manufacturer.* New York: McGraw-Hill.

Ohno, T. 1988. *Toyota Production System: Beyond Large-Scale Production.* New York: Productivity Press.

Public Affairs Division of Toyota. 1988. Toyota Motor Corporation.

Swartz, J.B. 1994. *The Hunters and the Hunted: A Non-Linear Solution for Reengineering the Workplace.* Portland, OR: Productivity Press.

PART II

IMPLEMENTATION

CHAPTER 4

The "Lean House" and Model Lines

OVERVIEW: Before embarking on a Lean improvement effort, healthcare leaders must first publicly declare their *intention* to really make it happen. Then they must develop a *vision* for the future organization. Next, leaders must build an *infrastructure* that will support and enhance the implementation of Lean. But first, they must understand the major components of Lean—the "Lean House." Before applying Lean to the entire healthcare system, leaders should demonstrate its effectiveness through *model lines.* To be effective, leaders also must learn to look at their organizations through a new set of eyes.

THE IMPORTANCE OF INFRASTRUCTURE

Healthcare organizations are not much different from other business entities in terms of what they spend their time doing. An inordinate amount of time is spent on non–value-added activities (e.g., rework, firefighting) but little time is spent on improvement. A major reason for the lack of attention to improvement activities, along with all-too-common organizational inertia, is that the *improvement infrastructure* doesn't exist. In fact, in my experience, healthcare organizations generally lack even a basic understanding of the concept of infrastructure, a failing that has made it nearly impossible for them to achieve long-term improvement.

What do I mean by "infrastructure?" My Merriam-Webster dictionary defines infrastructure as "the underlying foundation or basic framework of a system or organization." In other words, it's what makes the organization tick—how the organization functions and how robust and flexible it is to meet the challenges of an increasingly demanding competitive environment.

Success in applying Lean operations to your organization depends on an infrastructure that can support and nurture them. For our purposes, the Lean infrastructure includes a compelling vision; an organizational structure; a strategic plan; a management system; and a Lean knowledge base of Lean leaders, educated

---

Figure 4.1 Graphic of Virginia Mason's Strategic Plan

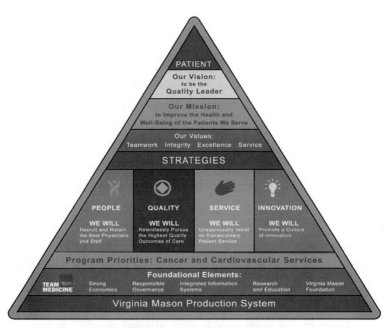

Source: Virginia Mason Medical Center. Used with permission.

---

employees, and consultants. *This infrastructure must be one that employees have a role in building, which gives them a sense of ownership.* We will be discussing the Lean infrastructure in the next three chapters along with the basic components of Lean, as represented by the "Lean House," or the Global Production System (GPS).

The creation of a new infrastructure to transform an organization to Lean requires different thinking. Boeing's Japanese *senseis* said, "Quick and crude is better than slow and elegant." In other words, getting your people started on something manageable they can do themselves is better than spending a great deal of time developing elaborate plans from the top that don't get people involved. They must be participants in the process.

So what constitutes the Lean infrastructure and what must happen before any plans can be deployed to change to it?

1. *A publicly declared intention by the leadership to move forward, to really make it happen.* Leaders of Virginia Mason made such a commitment with the rollout of a new strategic plan in 2001 (Figure 4.1).

   We were intrigued and impressed with the promise of Lean. We thought we had found a system with great promise in eliminating waste. Later in the year, we developed and approved a new strategic plan that had the right order to it: Patient First, Quality Leader, Best People, Best Service, and an environment of Innovation. In that plan, we committed to a Lean management philosophy for the entire organization (Kaplan and Rona 2003).

2. *A passionate, expansive, and publicly declared patient-first vision to deliver world-class-level healthcare without excuses and without waste.* Here's how I might word such a vision:

   The patient comes first, not we, the clinicians. Make no mistake about it; we are the patient's stewards. We are in the exclusive business of delivering world-class-level healthcare without waste.

Waiting is bad. We commit to delivering healthcare using waste-free processes, with passion and care for patient safety from the beginning of treatment to the end.

We will aggressively pursue defect-free medicine. Our job is to ensure our patients are not harmed in any way. This means rigorous accountability from the CEO to the janitor sweeping the floors.

We will be diligent in not adding new resources. Our job is to be attentive stewards of our resources. We will work to honor the following principles of good stewardship: spend no money, create no additional space, add no people, purchase no large machines, eliminate all unnecessary inventory. We will work every day using the tools of Lean to identify and eliminate waste. We will strive to deliver defect-free healthcare just in time.

We will be focused on meeting patient requirements for world-class quality service and do it just in time. The entire chain of command will be focused on where the work is being done, not in the executive offices. The care of our patients is our only priority. Our spirit every day will be driven by a spirit of improvement with a positive "can-do" attitude. Above all, we will approach the care of our patients and our daily work with urgency. We are in a crisis and must act now. Time is short.

3. *An understanding of the Global Production System or "Lean House."* The Global Production System is a generic representation of the Toyota Production System (TPS), as developed by Yoshiki Iwata and Chichiro Nakao of Shingijutsu Global Consulting, described graphically in Figure 4.2. I also refer to it as the "Lean House." Although initially conceived as a model for manufacturing, the Lean House also works well for healthcare, as I will explain by frequently making reference to healthcare terms and examples.

Global Production System (Lean House): A generic and graphic representation of the Toyota Production System (Lean)

Figure 4.2 The Global Production System, or Lean House

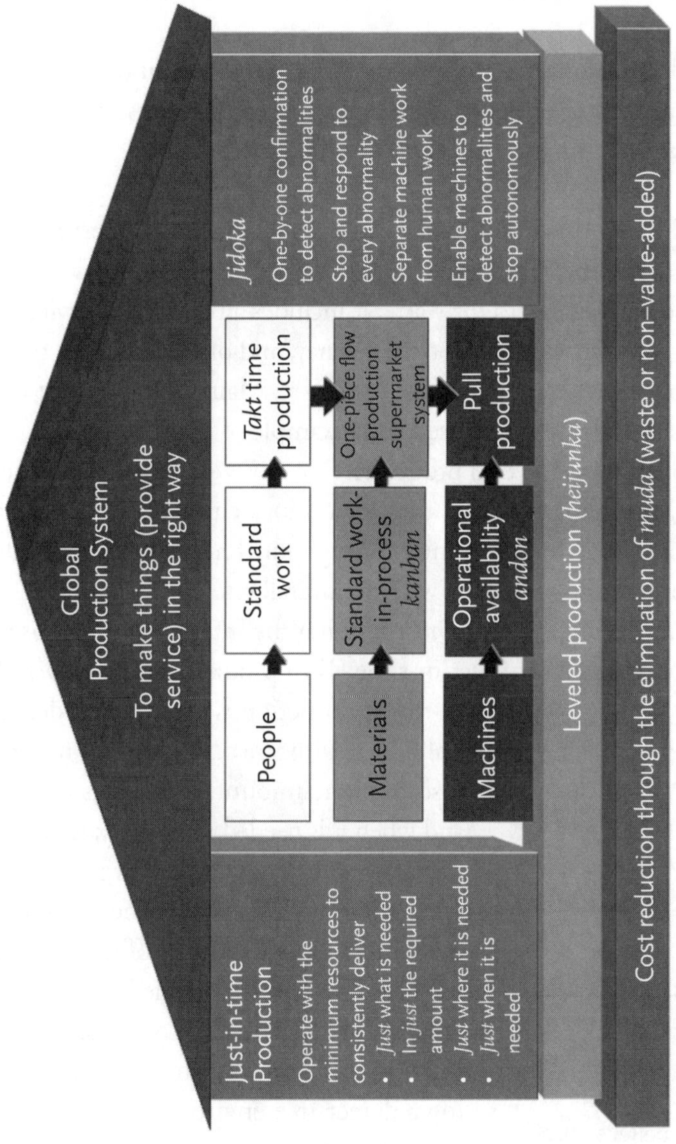

Global Production System

To make things (provide service) in the right way

Just-in-time Production

Operate with the minimum resources to consistently deliver

- *Just* what is needed
- In *just* the required amount
- *Just* where it is needed
- *Just* when it is needed

People | Standard work | *Takt* time production

Materials | Standard work-in-process *kanban* | One-piece flow production supermarket system

Machines | Operational availability *andon* | Pull production

Jidoka

One-by-one confirmation to detect abnormalities

Stop and respond to every abnormality

Separate machine work from human work

Enable machines to detect abnormalities and stop autonomously

Leveled production (*heijunka*)

Cost reduction through the elimination of *muda* (waste or non–value-added)

COMPONENTS OF THE LEAN HOUSE

The Lean House is made up of these major components: a foundation, a floor, two pillars, the resources and processes that go into the system (the interior), and a roof.

- The foundation—the *goal* of Lean—is continuous cost reduction through the elimination of waste. *Muda*, as mentioned earlier, is the Japanese word for waste; it includes all activities, services, and supplies that consume time, money, and other resources, but add no value to the delivery of healthcare. Maintaining patient information that is never used is an example of *muda*.
- The floor is "leveled production" or *heijunka*. Leveled production is scheduling products and services in such a way as to eliminate bottlenecks and maximize throughput. This includes scheduling patients in accordance with the overall rate of demand.
- Supporting the roof and enclosing the interior of the house are the two pillars of just-in-time (JIT) production and *jidoka*. Just-in-time production is consistently delivering only the healthcare service that is needed, in just the right amount, where it is needed, and when it is needed. In surgery, for example, that means providing the surgeon the correct instrument exactly when it is needed.
- *Jidoka* is the dual concept of maximizing the use of machines (in the healthcare environment, generally comprising medical equipment and technology) and creating a defect-free environment, where any employee can "stop the line" rather than passing a defect along the process. For example, if a nurse realizes that a patient has not had vital signs checked, the nurse should keep the patient from proceeding with further treatment.

> **Heijunka:** Scheduling products and services in such a way as to eliminate bottlenecks and maximize throughput

> **Stop the line:** Where any staff member can stop any process or procedure if that staff member believes proceeding would adversely affect patient safety or negatively impact efficient operations

- Within the house are three columns representing
  - the necessary resources of people, materials (supplies), and machines (left column);
  - the Lean methods of standard work, standard work-in-process/*kanban*, and *andon*/operational availability (middle column); and

> ***Takt* time:** production time aligned with demand

  - the outputs (or principles) of *takt* time (production time aligned with rate of demand), one-piece flow, and pull production (right column).
- The roof caps the whole system and integrates it behind the goal of providing services in the *right way* (i.e., the most efficient way).

This simple model can always be used by a team or an organization to focus or refocus on what they're doing and what they're trying to accomplish. Now let's examine each component in more detail.

Heijunka (the Floor)

Efficiency in a service organization, as in a manufacturing organization, requires that all parts of the organization operate in harmony with each other (i.e., not creating bottlenecks and backups for upstream or downstream operations). In the case of healthcare, bottlenecks and backups lead to unnecessary patient wait times, wasted time on the part of clinicians, and equipment underutilization.

Leveled production (*heijunka*), on the other hand, enables the organization not only to efficiently meet current demand, but even to meet increased demand. Leveled production results from studying organizational processes and their related outcomes to determine:

- the sequential steps in the process,
- how much time each step in the process takes,

- the process steps to allocate to each person in the process, and
- the total cycle time for the process.

Leveled production also helps determine staffing levels.

Just-in-Time Production and *Jidoka* (the Pillars)

Through a JIT healthcare delivery system, cost is minimized by revealing and eliminating waste embedded in the system. This enables the organization to operate with the minimum resources required in terms of people, supplies, and machines. In surgery, you don't want the surgeon waiting for the patient to arrive or vice versa when either is ready to begin an operation. And you don't want the nurse to hand the surgeon the instrument to begin a procedure before the surgeon is ready for it or, alternatively, have to hunt for the instrument at the last second.

Jidoka reveals abnormalities and problems in the delivery system by making inconsistent results immediately obvious. Employees are empowered to notice the inconsistency, stop the line (or process), and correct the problem, keeping the error from multiplying or compounding. An example is VMMC's Patient Safety Alert System, where any employee can stop any patient care process if she detects a defect or abnormality. By implementing such fail-safe processes, not only can your healthcare system attain the highest degree of patient safety, but it can achieve significant reductions in patient complaints and provider-related lawsuits.

Jidoka also includes the concept of *intelligently* determining which activities are best performed by people and which by machines. Do you want a lab technician to spend hours analyzing a blood sample or can it be done more quickly and accurately by a blood-testing device? Do you want to transmit patient charts from location to location by driver and van or electronically from computer to computer?

By understanding the concepts of JIT and *jidoka*, employees are empowered to improve their own processes and make them smoother and more efficient. Everyone is tuned in to noticing wasted space, time, and process steps, and finding ways to eliminate them or finding ways to use equipment and technology where it improves efficiency and patient care.

The Three Key Principles Within the House

Entering the Lean House, we see nine boxes in three columns. Moving from left to right, the columns represent in total the major resources, methods, and principles that enable JIT, *jidoka*, and leveled production (*heijunka*), resulting in the elimination of waste. I would like to first draw your attention to the right-hand column and elaborate on the three key principles of a Lean infrastructure for healthcare or any other industry.

1. Takt-*time-paced production*. This means providing products and services at the overall rate of demand from patients (*takt* time). For example, imagine that overall patient demand—or market demand—is for 40 patient visits per healthcare provider in an eight-hour day (480 minutes). Let's say 60 minutes of any provider's day is taken up with breaks, meetings, and other planned time when she is not available for patient care. That leaves 420 minutes. To meet patient demand, the provider would need to complete a patient visit every 10.5 minutes (420 minutes ÷ 40 patients) to meet the market demand. This is "*takt* time." *Takt* time makes leveled production (*heijunka*) possible.

2. *One-piece flow*. This is the opposite of "batching work." In one-piece flow, all equipment, other supplies, and information are physically grouped together to enable one person to perform all the steps necessary to complete a process or action. This system eliminates wasted time

> **One-piece flow:** In one-piece flow, all equipment, other supplies, and information are physically grouped together to enable one person to perform all the steps necessary to complete a process or action. It is the opposite of batching work.

between operations, paperwork, and unnecessary scheduling, while delivering a streamlined flow of products or services to meet customer needs. For a healthcare facility example, instead of serving many patients and then queuing them up for the next step in the process, patients proceed one step at a time through the process without delay or interruption.

3. *Pull production.* In pull production the pull is determined by the customer—in this case, the patient. "Pull" means that patients are processed only when they have requested a product or service (or are ready to receive it). This approach prevents providing service that is not required and eliminates needless waiting time. Once you have a predictable pace of service, one-piece flow, and standard work in place, a healthcare system can operate in a pull-production manner, enabling it to provide services when the patient needs them.

Lean Operations, Methods, and Principle Outputs

Now let's take a look at the three resources in the system (the left column)—people, materials, and machines—and identify what Lean methods (the middle column) support these resources, and, with long-term application, achieve the principle outputs of the Lean healthcare delivery system.

- Appropriate and efficient use of people's skills
  Method: *Standard work* is a prescribed, repeatable sequence of steps (or actions) that balances people's work to *takt* time. (See more detailed explanation below.)
  Principal output: *Takt*-time production, as described previously.
- Appropriate and minimal use of materials
  Methods: *Standard work-in-process* (SWIP) and *kanban* (sign boards) help balance the production and movement of materials to *takt* time and contribute to leveled production. Efficient SWIP is using the minimal amount of work-in-process inven-

tory (e.g., supplies) on the floor to provide patient care for the day. *Kanban* systems signal when to order more supplies, treat another patient, or move a patient or product to another area.

Standard work-in-process: The amount of work-in-process inventory on the floor to provide patient care for the day

Principal output: These methods work with *takt*-time management to enable one-piece flow.

- Appropriate and optimal use of machines
  Method: *Operational availability* and use of *andon* (visual alert or control) signals. Operational availability, achieved through preventive- and predictive-maintenance programs, ensures all types of healthcare equipment (e.g., electrocardiogram and magnetic resonance imaging machines) are available when they are needed. Machines and people use *andon* to signal an automatic or manual line stop.

Operational availability: The availability of healthcare equipment when needed

Andon systems also can be used to signal abnormal conditions and avoid overproduction by ensuring all output is usable.
Principal output: *Pull production.* Reliable equipment and one-piece flow enable synchronous, system-wide pull production without wasteful downtime and without the need to reschedule patients due to machines breaking down or being out of use.

Standard Work Elaborated

One of the most important concepts within Lean operations is "standard work." Put simply, standard work means *standardizing work to a repeatable cycle time*. For example, a process (e.g., a patient visit) should be satisfactorily completed in a certain amount of time (cycle time) to meet market demand (*takt* time). This requires identifying each step in a process and who should perform each step, as well as assigning a reasonable (repeatable) amount of time to complete each step. Figure 4.3 shows a standard work sheet health providers at PNHS use to identify the steps they must take to measure a patient's blood pressure.

Figure 4.3 Park Nicollet Standard Work Sheet for Blood Pressure Measurement

Standard Work	**Name of Activity:** Automatic Blood Pressure Measurement **Role Performing Activity:** Nursing Support Staff		
	Location: All sites except Creekside		**Department:** Internal Medicine/Family Medicine
	Document Owner: Director of Ambulatory Nursing, Georgene Sorensen, RN		
	Date Prepared: 9/28/2006	**Last Revision:** 8/28/2007	**Date Approved:**

Standard Work Summary: Process for obtaining an automated blood pressure measurement in the clinic by nursing support staff when initial blood pressure reading is greater than 130/80 for patients with diabetes or greater than 140/90 for patients without diabetes.

Task Sequence	Task Definition	Task Cycle Time (min)
1.	Obtain automated blood pressure unit.	00:15
2.	Instruct patient on procedure using the patient education form.	00:15
3.	Apply appropriately sized cuff to the patient's bare arm and align the artery position mark with the brachial artery.	00:26
4.	Press "On/Off" button to turn on automated blood pressure unit.	00:02
5.	Press "Start" button to begin three-minute countdown before cuff inflation of first blood pressure measurement and start timer.	00:02
6.	Instruct patient to do the following: a. Remain seated and do not cross legs. b. Do not talk during measurement. c. Keep arm resting on a solid surface so the inner aspect of the bend of the elbow is level with the heart. *The automated unit will turn off 5 minutes after the average measurement is calculated if it is running on its battery.	00:10
7.	Automated machine obtains three readings and produces an average reading.	06:00
8.	Return to room, obtain average measurement from automated unit, and remove cuff from patient's arm.	00:20
9.	Record blood pressure in electronic medical record and select the name of the automated unit in the comment drop-down box.	00:20

Source: Park Nicollet Health Services. Used with permission.

The two main purposes of standard work are: 1) to ensure work and expectations are safe and reasonable, and 2) to define and standardize normal conditions so abnormal conditions reveal themselves as soon as they occur.

As with any Lean process, there is a standard method for developing standard work. The most important tools are keen eyes and an inquisitive mind. Other tools may include a stopwatch and a video camera. These enable you to accurately measure the time each step in a process takes over and over until a repeatable average time can be determined. Standard work is *always* observed where it is performed, not developed in an office.

Standard work, along with SWIP and *takt* time, form the three-legged stool of standard operations (Figure 4.4).

> **Standard work sheet:** A document identifying the steps necessary to complete a task, who should perform each step, and the reasonable (repeatable) amount of time to complete each step

Keeping Your Lean House Clean and Well Organized

Although it's not shown in the Lean House graphic (Figure 4.2), a key consideration in Lean operations is maintaining a clean, well-organized

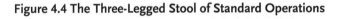

Figure 4.4 The Three-Legged Stool of Standard Operations

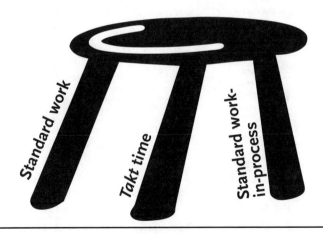

workplace. To do so, Lean employs what is known as a 5S process. The elements of this process follow and are further illustrated in Figure 4.5.

- *Sort.* Separate the necessary from the unnecessary by removing superflous tools, equipment, and procedures from the workplace.
- *Simplify.* Put everything in its place and organize material according to how frequently it is used, preferably with the help of visual aids.
- *Sweep.* Visually identify potential problems and deal with unsafe conditions or damaged equipment early in the process.
- *Standardize.* Define how a task should best be done and effectively communicate this to everyone involved. Document process changes as they occur.
- *Self-discipline.* Ensure that all housekeeping policies are adhered to by everyone. (This usually paves the way for success in other quality-improvement efforts.)

Figure 4.5 The 5S Process to Organize the Workplace

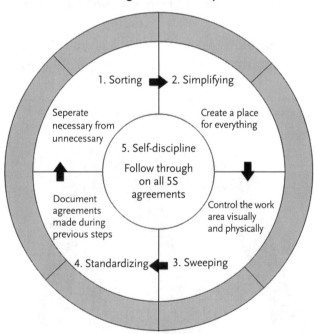

Creating Synergy

When all the elements represented in the Lean House work together, this synergy results in a systems approach that operates as an organic, living organization, optimizing talent and resources to deliver high-quality patient care. This system also creates a powerful cycle of continuous improvement. Here's how:

- Just-in-time production reveals abnormalities and problems in the production system and feeds this information to the *jidoka* system.
- Through *jidoka*, staff responds by stopping the process and installing a countermeasure that improves the entire system.
- Adjustments to the system (e.g., countermeasures and productivity improvements) establish a new standard for consistency in the JIT pillar.

The long-term benefits are decreased cost, increased morale, increased safety for patients and staff, higher-quality patient care, and, ultimately, zero defects.

THE IMPORTANCE OF ESTABLISHING A MODEL SERVICE LINE

Obviously, implementing Lean as represented by the Lean House illustration doesn't happen overnight. Attempting to improve the entire system all at once is not a good idea. As I've stressed, change is difficult and takes commitment, time, and other resources.

It's important not to bite off more than your organization can chew. However, achieving some immediate success stories as proof of the efficacy of the Lean approach is just as important. The best way to accomplish this is through a *model service line*, in other words, implementing the Lean infrastructure in one of your service lines (e.g., primary care, surgery, or cancer).

In the case of a model service line, you want world-class healthcare delivered with the basics: positive outcomes, a world-class standard of continuum of care, and a continuously improved value stream for the patient. The essential elements for developing a model service line are:

- understanding the future state of the business and the associated goals and metrics to achieve it;
- applying the right resources and the right tools to achieve the three key principles of *takt*-time-paced delivery, one-piece flow, and pull production; and
- putting the following model-line attributes in place:
  - standard work,
  - an ongoing 5S program,
  - no patients in queue,
  - seeing patients on demand,
  - reducing non–value-added clinician work,
  - increasing patient satisfaction continuously,
  - managing visibly on a daily basis (see Chapter 5),
  - aligning schedule with *takt* time,
  - leveling production (*heijunka*),
  - standardizing work-in-process,
  - enabling mistake proofing,
  - establishing a *kanban* system (see Chapter 8), and
  - ensuring patients are pulled, not pushed, through the system.

Developing a Lean model line means looking at the entire set of processes and activities necessary to provide a healthcare service from the time it is requested to the time it is provided. This is known as the *value stream* and it can be visually illustrated on what is known as a *value-stream map*, as demonstrated in Figure 4.6.

Note that Figure 4.6 is a simple illustration of a *portion* of the current-state process for having a surgical specimen (biopsy) analyzed for possible pathology (disease). In this case, the physician orders a test.

Figure 4.6. A Value-Stream Map Showing a Portion of the Process Involved in Testing a Surgical Specimen for Disease

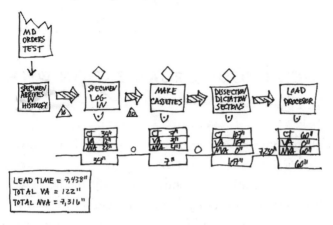

Source: Virginia Mason Medical Center. Used with permission.

The specimen (tissue) is sent to histology and logged into the laboratory system [log in cycle box]. Small plastic cassettes (containers) for holding the tissues are labeled with appropriate patient information [make cassettes cycle box]. A gross description of the specimen is then dictated as the specimen is being sectioned (dissected) [dissection, dictation, sections cycle box]. The sectioned tissues are placed into the previously labeled cassettes and the cassettes are loaded into the tissue processor where the tissues are preserved to make them ready for slide preparation and analysis [load processor cycle box].

Although some lead time is still involved in transporting the specimen from the doctor to histology, the bulk of the lead time shown of 7,438 seconds (or about 2 hours and 4 minutes), represents an improvement of 71 percent over the previous lead time of 25,627 seconds (or about 7 hours and 12 minutes). This is not shown in the figure.

Each part of the model line must be Lean. By understanding how all of the processes affect each other, we can apply Lean practices strategically, leveraging improvement opportunities and

> **Value-stream map:** A pictorial representation of the steps in a value system, either as a current or future (desired) state

allowing value to flow freely and rapidly. Real-life examples of model lines from Virginia Mason and Park Nicollet can be found in Chapters 10 and 12.

LOOKING AT YOUR ORGANIZATION WITH A NEW SET OF EYES

Many of these concepts and terms are new to you. Hopefully, you're developing a good sense of how moving to Lean operations can improve your organization. You should also gain an idea of what the change effort implies—sort of an "aha" moment. Here is how David Wessner (2005), CEO of PNHS, described how his eyes were opened during his top team's first trip to Japan:

> We are looking at a changing perception of what our reality is by observing something very different here in Japan. We will come back with eyes that are different, that will be unable to look at the same things the same way that we have been. We will come back to Park Nicollet with different eyes that we would not have had if we had not made this trip. I think we are learning how we can gain energy from our obstacles as opposed to being defeated by our obstacles.

Now that you have the infrastructure to potentially deliver world-class healthcare, the next step is to create an action plan to make the improvements you desire—creating the fully functioning Lean healthcare organization. That's the subject of our next chapter.

CHAPTER TAKEAWAYS

- Before embarking on a Lean improvement effort, healthcare leaders must publicly declare their intention to really make it happen.

- They must then develop a vision for the future organization.
- Next, leaders must begin to build the *infrastructure* of Lean to support the components of Lean, as graphically represented by the Global Production System, or what the author calls the Lean House.
- The foundation of the Global Production System is eliminating waste (*muda*).
- Other key concepts are as follows:
  - leveled production (*heijunka*) where throughput is maximized and bottlenecks are eliminated,
  - just-in-time production, or JIT (only producing what's needed when and where it's needed),
  - *jidoka* (maximizing the use of machines and creating a defect-free environment),
  - standard work where work is standardized to a *repeatable* cycle time that is efficient and meets market demand (*takt* time),
  - standard work-in-process and *kanban* together minimize work-in-process inventory and signal when to order more supplies or take another action,
  - *andon* (visual alert/control),
  - *takt*-time production (production at the rate that matches patient demand),
  - one-piece flow (where a single worker handles all the steps of a process/action), and
  - pull production (where the patient determines when he needs a product or service).
- The 5S process keeps the workplace clean and well organized.
- Establishing model service lines not only helps demonstrate the power of Lean, but enables the organization to implement Lean one building block at a time.
- A value stream is the entire set of processes and activities necessary to provide a healthcare service from the time it is requested to when it is provided. A value-stream map shows the processes and activities graphically.

> • To be effective, a healthcare leader must learn to look at the organization "through a new set of eyes."

REFERENCES

Kaplan, G.S., and J.M. Rona. 2003. "Becoming a Lean Organization— Rekindling the Drive and the Passion." Virginia Mason Medical Center Letter to Executives, Seattle, Washington.

Wessner, D. 2005. Remarks to top team of Park Nicollet Health Services. Toyohashi, Japan, May 22.

CHAPTER 5

Your Lean Action Plan

OVERVIEW: As the healthcare leader, you must provide the foundation for a successful Lean implementation by emphasizing that the patient comes first and by truly believing you can succeed. In this chapter, the preparatory steps for and key elements of your action plan are described. The *Kaizen* Promotion Office will provide your primary help in implementing, evaluating, and adjusting your Lean action plan. You will also benefit from a world-class management system. Keep in mind that gaining traction with the plan starts with your leadership.

TWO FOUNDATIONAL REQUIREMENTS

As I've emphasized, the first thing you must do on the road to becoming a world-class healthcare organization is to focus on the patient. You, the leader, have to believe that the patient is top priority and demonstrate this by your actions. In a culture where the medical staff is often placed on a pedestal, putting the patient first may be a challenge. So it's important to state this priority in writing for all staff and patients to see. Below is the commitment the Toyota Memorial Hospital in Toyota City, Japan, made in a 2005 brochure:

We will have a "patient comes first" policy, prioritizing the right medical care and focusing on patient satisfaction. We pledge to heed the will of the patients, and endeavor to establish the Toyota Way unique to our Toyota Memorial Hospital, as a world-standard hospital that is open to the community and the world.

Second, you must *believe* that you can set and achieve "stretch" targets such as the following:

- Reduce lead times for patient care delivery and service from months to weeks to days to minutes to seconds—and do it defect free.
- Achieve quality gains of 10 times or better.
- Reduce space by 50 percent in two to three years.
- Increase gross profit by 10 percent (or more).
- Double in size in five years, using freed-up cash.

Why should you believe you can achieve such goals? Because, as you will see in Chapters 9 to 12, similar results have been achieved by other healthcare organizations that have implemented Lean.

PREPARATORY STEPS

Before you prepare the Lean action plan for your organization, there are certain things you must accomplish:

1. *Get rid of competing improvement strategies* (e.g., total quality management, organizational development, process management, process improvement, and Six Sigma). Lean production is all you need.
2. *Find an outside* sensei (master teacher) who can teach you how to eliminate waste. You want a master with a corporate operations track record who was trained by the Japanese and has deep knowledge of *kaizen*. Make sure the *sensei* has at

least 20 years of experience building a product and being responsible for a budget, and has implemented Lean operations. Ask your *senseis* how many times a day they "washed their hands" on their last job. ("Wash your hands" is the term used by some teachers to indicate spending time where the work is actually being done.)

3. *Sign nothing shorter than a five-year contract* with your consulting firm to prove to yourself that you're really going to do it. Then tell your *senseis* (the consultants) they have "air cover" so they can move forward aggressively. Experience shows that once you begin implementing Lean, you will receive phone calls from the "anchor draggers" (as we call them) in your organization who want to get rid of the *senseis*.

4. *Develop a sense of urgency* by seizing or creating a crisis (or crises) to get Lean implemented. Everybody in your organization, from the top of the chain of command to the bottom, may dismiss the idea that there's a crisis or any urgency needed. How could there be? Perhaps you've been told for years that your hospital system is listed as one of the top 100 hospitals in the United States. Paying attention to such accolades amounts to "drinking your own bathwater."

The goal is a 50 percent reduction of all waste. Sound impossible? It has been accomplished by others and you can do it by creating and applying good value-stream maps and by following an unforgiving business plan based on tough, simple targets—e.g., cutting patient lead time in half every 12 months. The Japanese experts have taught us: "spend no money, add no people, buy no equipment, and create no additional space; just do *kaizen* every day."

ELEMENTS OF THE PLAN

Once you've committed to Lean, found your *sensei(s)*, and created a sense of urgency, you can develop your plan. Key elements are:

1. *Identify your business and its scope.* What do you exist to do? Is it to deliver defect-free healthcare? To make a profit? To provide employment for healthcare professionals? What are your core competencies? What specific products/services do you intend to provide and at what price?

2. *Establish a* Kaizen *Promotion Office and* Kaizen *Operations Teams.* The purpose of the *Kaizen* Promotion Office (KPO) and the *Kaizen* Operations Teams (KOTs) is to promote and manage all improvement activities in the system. (See "The *Kaizen* Promotion Office and *Kaizen* Operations Teams" later in this chapter.)

3. *Begin with a model line an inch wide and a mile deep.* To demonstrate the power of Lean, you must quickly produce a success story. Most organizations implementing Lean tend to want to start everywhere. However, starting everywhere is a mistake. With the counsel of your *sensei*, you must first determine your main value stream—usually the hospital itself.

   Drilling down, the hospital is fed by the operating room, so the surgery department drives the process. This department provides a golden opportunity for *heijunka* and taking out waste. It can also be the toughest place to start if the chief of surgery and the surgeons resist signing on as progressive champions and leaders of the process.

4. *Implement your waste-elimination strategy through workplace* kaizen *events and* kaikaku *(broad scale and radical improvement).* Apply workplace *kaizen* in the form of Rapid Process Improvement Workshops to eliminate waste in how work is done in individual work units. Apply *kaikaku* to powerfully reconfigure the entire value stream. (See "Implement Lean Through *Kaizen* Events and *Kaikaku*" later in this chapter.)

   Kaikaku: Broad-scale and radical improvement

5. *Map value streams, disrupt the organization.* Producing value-stream maps that show both the *as is* state and the 12-month *to be* state (the vision for the future) will produce shocks throughout the organization. Why? Because your people will

see that the surgery department, cancer department, primary clinics, and other functional silos are operating with a large percentage of *non–value-added* time and activities. The great majority of this *muda* (waste) can be eliminated with Lean operations. Your maps should be simple and focused on manageable portions of the process flow.

6. *Focus on cutting lead time and cycle time to meet* takt *time. Takt* time, defined in Chapter 4, is the key element in establishing continuous-flow production. It is *market driven* and must be met to improve patient satisfaction. (See "Cut Lead Time and Cycle Time to Meet *Takt* Time" later in this chapter.)

7. *Reorganize by service lines and value streams, and flatten the organization.* Turn the organization on its side to create a clear path from suppliers through the work processes of the company to patients. (See "Reorganize by Service Lines and Value Streams, and Flatten the Organization" later in this chapter.)

8. *Develop internal leaders with a passion for* kaizen. This is the subject of Chapter 6, "Building *Kaizen* Leaders."

9. *Deal with excess people at the outset.* Success in implementing Lean depends on devising a strategy to quickly identify and convert or remove the *anchor draggers*—those managers or other employees who won't give new ideas a fair trial. One way to accomplish this is by identifying leaders who can bring the doubters around. Within two years—after the ship is on a steadier course—it's time for the "Lean depth study." This study looks at various functions, as well as all levels of managers leading those functions, and eliminates those functions and managers determined to be non–value added. Offering early retirement is one tactic for dealing with excess personnel. Reassignment is another, provided that those people have bought into Lean and there is a value-added place to put them.

10. *Implement a world-class management system.* The three elements are management by policy (rather than objectives), daily management, and cross-functional management. (See "A

World-Class Management System to Make Your Plan Work"
later in this chapter.)
11. *Link pay to value creation and elimination of defects; install Lean
accounting.* Linking pay to value creation, as Toyota does, focuses
the entire workforce on eliminating waste and creating value.

WHAT IS LEAN ACCOUNTING?

Lean accounting is my term for merging Lean management principles, processes, and practices with the budgeting ideas of management experts Jeremy Hope and Robin Fraser, as set forth in their
2003 book *Beyond Budgeting: How Managers Can Break Free from
the Annual Performance Trap.* You can see this combined approach
in practice in organizations such as Park Nicollet Health Services.

The major difference between traditional budgeting and Lean
accounting is replacing fixed financial targets with targets based on
key performance indicators. For PNHS, there are two such targets:
1) cost per unit of service, and 2) units of service per full-time
equivalent (FTE). The traditional budgeting process is *eliminated.*
Among other consequences, staffing levels thus become a product of
the number of units of service provided.

According to David Cooke (2007), chief financial officer (CFO)
at PNHS:

> Under our old system, we began preparing next year's budget in
> July and many people spent almost all their time until October
> preparing a budget to present to our board in December. It was
> mainly a political document, explaining how revenues would be
> divvied up; it had nothing to do with incenting people to improve
> performance. Most of our managers have little to do with con-
> trolling revenue, but a lot to do with controlling production.

In particular, Cooke based PNHS's budgeting process on two
key concepts from Fraser and Hope (2003):

1. Under Lean accounting, the organization's current quarter performance is measured against its immediate past quarter performance. Also, each person's current quarter performance is measured against his performance in the same quarter of the past year. Doing this enables the measurement of *performance* improvement (or lack thereof). You can better judge people's performance by focusing on how they perform against themselves rather than focusing on how they perform against a fixed budget.
2. Budget forecasting is increased to encompass the next six quarters, not just the upcoming fiscal year. Adjustments are made based on the current quarter's performance and trend lines, making the budget more flexible and a more accurate predictor of results.

How do managers achieve a budget increase? Usually by improving their performance so that they stretch the same dollars further.

"By focusing on making incremental improvements rather than meeting budget targets, the organization unleashes the creativity of its people to do their best work," Cooke says.

THE *KAIZEN* PROMOTION OFFICE AND *KAIZEN* OPERATIONS TEAMS

The *Kaizen* Promotion Office (KPO) comprises the team that will:

- work with the CEO and top leadership to develop the Lean action plan;
- work with line managers on a day-to-day basis to ensure implementation (e.g., standard work);
- assist with the education and development of Lean leaders;
- help replicate and spread best practices;
- evaluate results and recommend adjustments to the plan, if necessary; and
- communicate successes.

You should put your best people in the KPO and have your *sensei* approve those you select. In addition, you should promote from within; you may not know it but you have bright, passionate people who will jump at the opportunity to join the KPO. Take only the best.

At Toyota, up to 5 percent of the workforce is assigned full time to *kaizen*. In fact, ever since I started going to Japan, beginning in 1990, the top 100 companies in Japan that fit the definition of *world class* all assign 2 to 5 percent of their workforce full time to *kaizen*. Establishing the KPO and then establishing a long-term infrastructure to support *kaizen* is the most important job you have as a healthcare leader, along with leading the effort.

The KPO should report directly to the CEO. To support the Lean effort, create *Kaizen* Operations Teams (KOTs) for each major service line and for corporate functions. A good example is the way Park Nicollet has organized its Lean effort (Figure 5.1).

Figure 5.1 The *Kaizen* Promotion Office Structure at Park Nicollet Health Services

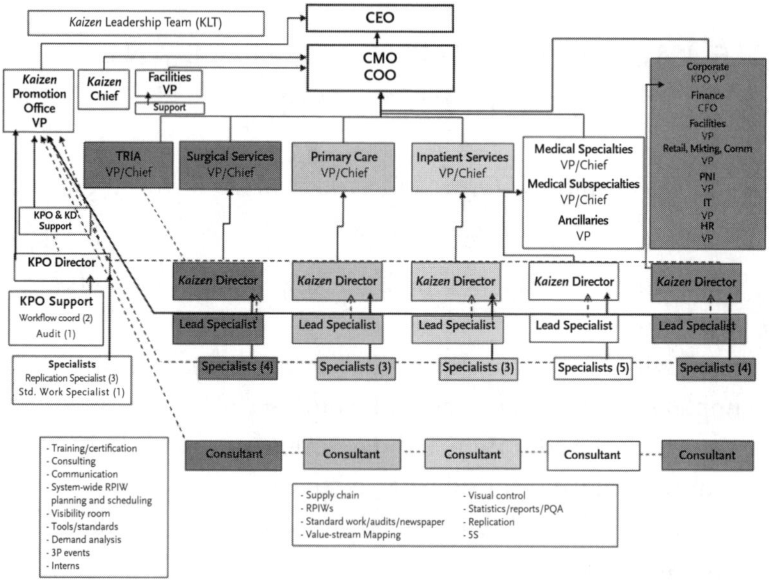

Source: Park Nicollet Health Services. Used with permission.

If you look at the boxes under the service lines (i.e., surgical services, primary care) and the box for corporate functions, you will see that each is supported by a KOT, with a director, a lead specialist, and several other specialists. Under the guidance of the KPO, these teams work with line managers and other clinicians to implement Lean.

All individuals occupying positions on the chart, starting with the CEO, are required to complete an 18-month Lean certification program. All positions with the exception of model-line leaders are expected to serve a minimum of three years in their positions. Model-line leaders are also the service-line leaders.

For example, the primary care model-line leaders are the chief of primary care and the senior vice president of primary care. They're supported by an executive with the title of *kaizen* director. All *kaizen* directors are executive leaders and lead a team of highly trained Lean specialists. All positions on the chart with the exception of the CEO, chief medical officer (CMO), chief operating officer (COO), and model-line leaders are dedicated full time to Lean.

The vice president of the KPO is responsible for alignment of all the tools of Lean. All *kaizen* directors and their teams report (on a dotted line) to the vice president of the KPO who, as stated and shown above, reports directly to the CEO.

IMPLEMENT LEAN THROUGH *KAIZEN* EVENTS AND *KAIKAKU*

We briefly mentioned *kaizen* events (or RPIWs) in Chapter 2. As stated there, a *kaizen* event is a team-based, disciplined, five-day process to eliminate waste using Lean tools. A *kaizen* event, as the name might imply, is a way of accelerating *kaizen* (continuous incremental improvement).

Sometimes, though, broad-scale and radical improvement is needed to change an entire value stream (i.e., when a new facility is required). The Japanese term for this is *kaikaku,* and one of its chief tools is the production preparation process (3P).

The purpose of 3P is to structure defect-free, world-class quality of care that can be delivered at the required patient-demand volume (*takt* time) just in time using simple and defect-free processes. The process starts with a blank sheet of paper, in most cases. Flexibility in thinking is required. The intent is to separate in your mind the focus on a particular physical space from the process you need to deliver world-class healthcare every day.

Start where and how the work gets done, and focus on non–value-added activities. The value-stream map (VSM) process will identify these. *Kaizen* tactics for determining specific projects are based on the VSMs. For example, a general surgery *current state* map might show the following for a patient having an operation:

> **3P:** Production preparation process

- Lead time = 4,453 minutes
- Cycle time = 88 minutes
- Value-added = 43 minutes
- Non–value added = 4,410 minutes (99 percent non–value added)

The *future state* map (what you want the patient visit to look like in 12 months) might look like this:

- Lead time = 2,992 minutes
- Cycle time = 90 minutes
- Value added = 52 minutes
- Non–value added = 2,940 minutes (98 percent non–valued added)

While the non–value-added percentage has only declined by 1 percentage point, the time the patient spends in process has been cut by 1,470 minutes, or 33 percent. Not a bad start for the *kaizen* journey. You don't improve by tackling value, you improve by eliminating waste (i.e., non–value-added activities, services, and supplies).

The use of 3P to reconfigure the value stream is only needed in the case of a greenfield or brownfield situation. "Greenfield" means repeated *kaizen* events over a period of time are not working and the process needs to be expanded considerably. For example, an entirely new clinic is required. "Brownfield" means that repeated *kaizen* dictates a completely different approach (*kaikaku*) and you must use 3P to reconfigure the flow dramatically in the existing space.

> **Greenfield:** A new facility or process
> **Brownfield:** An established facility or process

CUT LEAD TIME AND CYCLE TIME TO MEET *TAKT* TIME

Total lead time is the time taken to complete a patient care event, including processing time and waiting time. In other words, it's the time from when the patient requests service until the account is settled. Sometimes we focus on a subset of total lead time, such as day-of-service lead time or billing-cycle lead time.

Cycle time is measured with a stopwatch and comes in different categories. Operator cycle time is the time required for a single employee to complete one cycle of work. It includes the value-added time and the waste within the process step. It does *not* include waiting time before and after. The formula is:

> **Cycle time:** The amount of time it takes to complete a task or process

cycle time = value added + waste + value added + waste.

Cycle time is observed and standard work is used to improve it.

Takt time, as defined in Chapter 4, equals time available divided by output required. It is the key element in establishing continuous-flow production and is calculated independent of capacity, number of providers, process capability, etc. *Takt* time is *market driven* and must be met to improve patient satisfaction.

REORGANIZE BY SERVICE LINES AND VALUE STREAMS, AND FLATTEN THE ORGANIZATION

Perhaps the greatest example of *kaikaku* is reorganizing your entire healthcare system. *This is what I recommend.* All parts of your system, including your suppliers, should be in direct-line support of the patient, as in Figure 5.2.

This example shows three value streams: the operating room (OR), the hospital, and the overall healthcare enterprise. The product to deliver is defect-free surgery supported by synchronized flows of services and other resources coming from the hospital and the overall enterprise. Notice the straight horizontal line directly from where patients enter the system to where they exit and go home after

Figure 5.2 The Global Enterprise Value-Stream Network

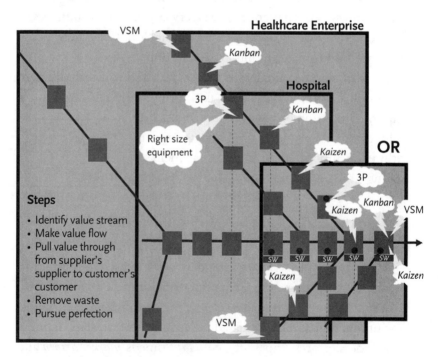

Note: VSM = value-stream mapping; SW = standard work; OR = operating room

surgery is completed. Traditional functional silos have been eliminated. The organization has been flattened.

In the Prototype Lean Organization (Figure 5.3), traditional vertical structures are eliminated. The business is defined in terms of delivery of service to the patient. The identification and channeling of the value stream for a family of products and services results in value flowing smoothly to the customer, that is, the patient.

Present-day healthcare organizations are inefficient and present obstacles to delivering value. They're organized around clinicians, procedures, and hospital administration, rather than around the patient. The anesthesiologists believe they are in the anesthesia business; a nephrology group sees itself as in the nephrology business; and so forth. Hospitals, to the extent that they think in terms of service lines, normally define them in terms of specialties (e.g., internal medicine, radiology, urology, surgery).

Model lines in the prototype Lean organization are the primary focus of Lean implementation and activity. All the tools of Lean and the KPO support are focused to optimize the seven flows of medicine (described in detail in Chapter 7) and eliminate defects. The model lines focus on aggressively burrowing into the many levels, an inch wide and a mile deep, attacking the seven wastes (as described in Chapter 2).

This model moves from the traditional vertical organization chart of command and control to a flatter organization that can respond to a dynamic environment. The goal of the Lean organization and its structure is to continuously improve in the areas of quality patient care, timeliness, responsiveness, and optimization of internal resources, based upon the demands of the healthcare environment. This goal is achieved through standard work processes and services with the focus on the relentless elimination of waste.

In Figure 5.3, the executive administrator/president and the CEO work with the macro-groups in the system: the support functions (e.g., finance, marketing, human resources), and the product/service families, which are illustrated vertically and on the bottom of the chart. The KPO reports directly to the CEO.

Figure 5.3 The Prototype Lean Organization

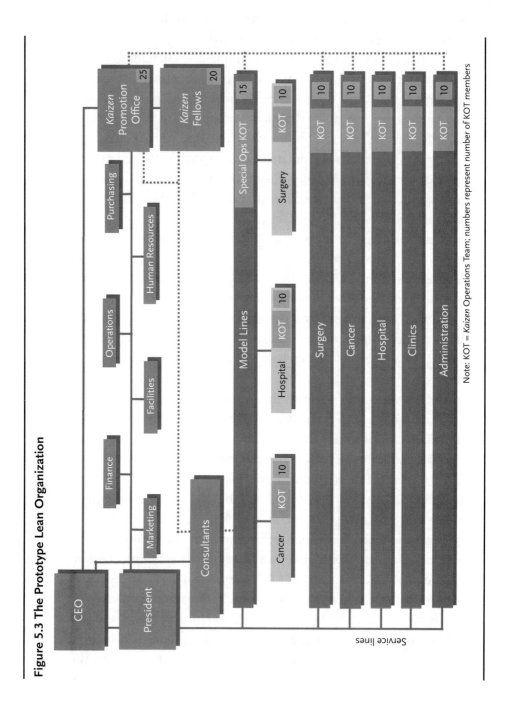

Note: KOT = *Kaizen Operations Team*; numbers represent number of KOT members

A major part of the KPO's function will be helping the organization move forward with highly detailed, five-year plans based on four five-year blocks of implementation (point, line, plane, cube). These stages collectively are known as the *kaizen* path (Figure 5.4)

For example, if your organization is in the first five-year block, your detailed yearly plans for the second five-year block (line) should be finalized and issued by year four of the first five-year block (point). Otherwise, you'll find yourself in a reactive mode rather than in the highly disciplined planning-and-implementation mode that should be the standard for providing world-class service.

Service Lines

The functions outlined in Figure 5.3 are the heart and soul of the service-delivery centers of the organization, in this example surgery center, cancer care center, hospital care, clinical care, and the administrative function. A service line is logically different from traditional departmental functions. A service line encompasses all activities that support and deliver services to the patient.

The primary responsibilities of a service line leader (SLL) are: a) to meet the production needs demanded by the market (*takt* time) using the resources provided by the healthcare organization, and b) to establish and document standard-work processes and their consistent application within the line. Since the market defines production and service needs, the resources that the SLL manages do not *belong* to him, but rather are *assigned to him by the organization* and can be redeployed based on market demand. An SLL knows and respects this because doing so provides better service delivery to the patient population and optimizes resources within the system. Team members can then deliver the right skills, at the right time, in the right amount.

Figure 5.4 The *Kaizen* Path

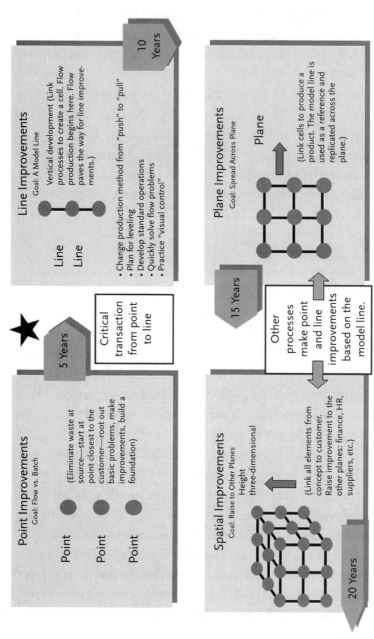

Point Improvements
Goal: Flow vs. Batch

Point

Point

Point

(Eliminate waste at source—start at point closest to the customer—root out basic problems, make improvements, build a foundation)

5 Years ★

Critical transaction from point to line

Line Improvements
Goal: A Model Line

Line
Line

Vertical development (Link processes to create a cell. Flow production begins here. Flow paves the way for line improvements.)

- Change production method from "push" to "pull"
- Plan for leveling
- Develop standard operations
- Quickly solve flow problems
- Practice "visual control!"

10 Years

Spatial Improvements
Goal: Raise to Other Planes

Height three-dimensional

(Link all elements from concept to customer. Raise improvement to the other planes: finance, HR, suppliers, etc.)

20 Years

Other processes make point and line improvements based on the model line.

Plane Improvements
Goal: Spread Across Plane

Plane

(Link cells to produce a product. The model line is used as a reference and replicated across the plane.)

15 Years

Source: Originally published as *Jysauto in taimo seisan kakumei shido manyuaru*/copyright © 1989 by JIT Management Library Company, Ltd., Tokyo, Japan. English translation copyright © 1990 Productivity Press, an imprint of Taylor & Francis Group, an Informa Business www.ProductivityPress.com.

Supporting Functions

At the top part of this organization chart, we find finance, operations, purchasing (or materials management), marketing, facilities (or engineering), and human resources. Their main task is to support the service lines by providing the necessary resources for them, and by standardizing and controlling procedures as they apply to them. Leaders of the support functions must work together with the SLLs to create and sustain standard procedures within the service lines.

Standardization of work at all levels is important because it:

- enables constant step-by-step improvements through the ongoing *kaizen* activities in the medical center;
- enables the medical center to better employ its resources (through internal flexibility) to respond to the realities of the market;
- enables staff members to acquire and develop their knowledge and skills in a balanced and objective manner;
- makes processes more transparent (and therefore more efficient); and
- makes better use of personnel by involving staff members in the decisions and activities that impact their processes.

A WORLD-CLASS MANAGEMENT SYSTEM TO MAKE YOUR PLAN WORK

Perhaps the most critical piece of the Lean infrastructure is establishing a "world-class management system" to operate your organization. This world-class management system consists of three elements:

1. *Daily management:* The system used by an organization to perform its daily activities by establishing standard operations; eliminating waste in work methods; and using facts and data

to ensure that process, products, and services are continuously improved and always predictable.

Daily management serves as the basis for:

- knowing the level of performance of important areas by organizational units as well as for the whole company;
- determining areas of breakthrough for the management by policy (MBP) system; and
- determining improvement priorities for all important areas throughout the organization. Priority categories are:
  - needs breakthrough improvement (MBP),
  - needs incremental improvement (daily),
  - requires effort to maintain "as is"—do not allow progress to deteriorate (daily), and
  - necessitates work to hold the gains of breakthrough achievement from the MBP system.

2. *Management by policy:* How goals are determined, how plans to achieve the goals are established, and how measures are created to ensure progress toward the goals. MBP is the opposite of management by objectives (MBO). MBP is a *catch-ball process*, meaning that, starting with the CEO, goals are proposed and discussed by people all the way down and up the chain of command. MBP is a highly participative process, as contrasted with MBO, which is directive and not based on ensuring that the proposed targets can be achieved or that the chain of command has the means to do so. Top management takes the initiative, but confers throughout the system with subordinate managers and genuinely takes their views and all of their data into account.

> **Catch-ball process:** Where goals are proposed and discussed by people all the way down and up the chain of command

Top management also
- reviews and analyzes internal data from customers,
- assesses the competitive environment,

- examines internal data from the daily management process, and
- compares these data with the company's vision and long-term planning in order to develop goals.

Management by policy (*hoshin kanri*) gives high visibility to individual and group accountabilities. Leaders use it to deploy and emphasize policies. Goals are quantified, methods of achieving the goals are clearly communicated, and roles and expectations are agreed upon before action is taken. Regular diagnoses and reviews are conducted to measure both progress toward goals and the effectiveness of the methods employed. Figure 5.5 provides an illustration of the process.

Figure 5.5 The Three Elements of Management by Policy: Policy Development, Policy Deployment, and Diagnosis and Review

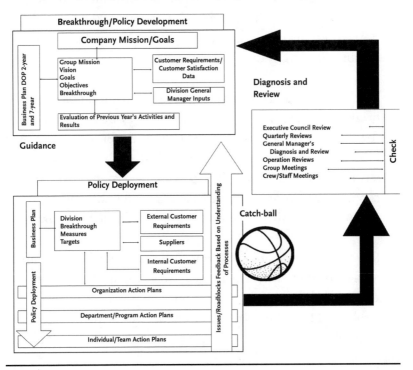

Figure 5.6 General Sequence for Implementing the World-Class Management System

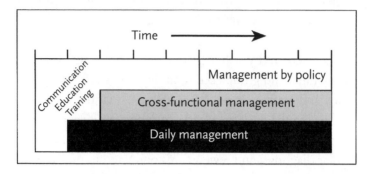

3. *Cross-functional management:* The major management system for implementing breakthrough improvements across organizational lines. Cross-functional management is always focused on the elements of full customer satisfaction. At the group level, leadership determines potential breakthroughs using the MBP process. At the division level (or another level), division management identifies the breakthroughs.

   Cross-functional management can be used to implement a breakthrough, so long as necessary resources are available. An "owner" (usually a senior executive) leads the breakthrough. A formal process is established to make sure major customer-satisfaction needs are met. The parts of the system involved cooperate and coordinate the balancing and prioritizing of resources and activities needed to implement the breakthrough.

World-class companies recognize the need for proper implementation of such a management system. Figure 5.6 depicts the general sequence for implementation. Daily management comes first, followed by either MBP or cross-functional management (or both simultaneously). All are implemented starting with communication, education, and training.

Until daily management and cross-functional management are in place, MBP will not work to its maximum potential.

VISIBILITY ROOM AND WEEKLY STAND-UP MEETINGS

Another element critical to embedding Lean in the organization is a *visibility room* that houses the organization's transformational business plan. The leadership team meets in this room to review strategy.

The visibility room provides a constantly available location to easily view, through charts posted on the wall, the organization's Lean implementation progress. For example, metrics for each model line scheduled for, or undergoing, Lean implementation are posted. Top measures—what we learned in Japan in the 1990s—are quality, cost, delivery, safety, and morale (QCDSM), updated quarterly. Figure 5.7 shows the information posted on a wall in Park Nicollet's visibility room.

At the next level, progress in the tactics for achieving success in the overall strategy is reported in a weekly stand-up meeting chaired by the CEO. The meeting is preferably conducted early in the week and early in the morning, before the official workday starts. All Lean leaders stand up and report progress toward goals, problems being addressed, and countermeasures being taken.

The weekly stand-up meeting must be mandatory and never cancelled. Such meeting systems are in place at Virginia Mason and at Park Nicollet, as Figures 5.8 and 5.9 demonstrate.

GAINING TRACTION WITH THE PLAN—IT STARTS WITH YOU

I've identified all the elements of your Lean action plan. Now let's talk about how to gain traction with it. You gain traction by

Figure 5.7

Park Nicollet's visibility room.

Source: Park Nicollet Health Services. Used with permission.

Figure 5.8

Virginia Mason's former president Mike Rona (right) and CEO Gary Kaplan leading a stand-up meeting.

Source: Virginia Mason Medical Center. Used with permission.

Figure 5.9

Dr. Steve Connelly, chief of surgical services at Park Nicollet Health Services, presents the status of Lean progress in surgical services at a weekly stand-up meeting covering Lean progress on all service lines as CEO David Wessner (immediately left of Connelly) listens.

Source: Park Nicollet Health Services. Used with permission.

spending time on the hospital floor (the *gemba*, where the work gets done) and listening to your people (who know where the waste is and who want it eliminated). You

> *Gemba:* Where the work gets done, e.g., the factory or hospital floor

have to demonstrate your commitment and observe how the work is actually performed by walking the floor *every day.* Doing so also helps you develop a good eye for different kinds of waste. Leading the change effort also requires the following:

- *A top-down focus on the details.* Delegation doesn't work. The devil is in the details and so is the payoff.
- *An engaged chain of command.* This encompasses all leaders from the CEO to first-line supervisors, all of whom understand that their future success depends on thoroughly

embracing and implementing Lean in everyday management.

- *Creating effective value-stream maps, correctly focused and flaw-lessly executed RPIWs, and achievable targets.* These are all linked to metrics driven by Lean accounting. Lean accounting identifies activities that add value and those that don't.

It's not easy to implement Lean. It takes time, commitment, stamina, strong leadership, and a significant investment. However, successful implementation will pay huge dividends in improved operations, min-imized waste and defects, and increased patient and staff satisfaction— all enhancing your organizational reputation, winning you new patients, and solidifying your leadership position in today's increasingly competitive healthcare environment.

CHAPTER TAKEAWAYS

As the healthcare leader, you must provide the foundation for a successful Lean implementation by, first, emphasizing that the patient comes first and, second, truly believing you can succeed.

There are four preparatory steps your should take when preparing your Lean action plan:

- Get rid of competing improvement strategies.
- Find an outside *sensei* (master teacher) to teach you how to apply Lean.
- Sign at least a five-year contract with your consulting firm.
- Create a *sense of urgency* to get Lean implemented.

Your plan should:

- Identify your business and its scope.
- Establish a *Kaizen* Promotion Office (KPO) and *Kaizen*

Operations Teams (KOTs) to promote and manage all
improvement activities in the system.

- Begin with a model line an inch wide and a mile deep.
- Implement your waste-elimination strategy through work-place *kaizen* events and *kaikaku* (broad-scale and radical improvement).
- Map value streams; disrupt the organization.
- Focus on cutting lead time and cycle time to meet *takt* time.
- Reorganize by service lines and value streams, and flatten the organization.
- Develop internal leaders with a passion for *kaizen*.
- Deal with excess people at the outset.
- Implement a world-class management system.
- Gear pay to value creation and eliminating defects; install "Lean accounting."
- Implement a world-class management system to make your plan work.

REFERENCES

Hope, J., and R. Fraser. 2003. *Beyond Budgeting: How Managers Can Break Free from the Annual Performance Trap*. Cambridge, MA: Harvard Business School Press.

Toyota Memorial Hospital. 2005. "Brochure." p. 1.

CHAPTER 6

Building *Kaizen* Leaders

OVERVIEW: This chapter examines what's required of Lean leaders and how to build them, including how to enlist physicians in the cause of implementing Lean. A typical Lean certification (i.e., education) program is described, as are two steps to drive Lean deeper into your organization. A number of obstacles leaders may encounter as they implement Lean are identified, along with potential solutions.

SUCCESSFUL LEAN IMPLEMENTATION REQUIRES THE RIGHT LEADERS

The last chapter covered the elements of your organization's Lean action plan and some of what is required to carry it out. In this chapter, I want to focus on the role of leadership among four groups: top leaders, members of the *Kaizen* Promotion Office (KPO), line administrative managers (including those who are physicians), and physicians in general. Second, I will describe how to educate these groups and drive them toward becoming *Lean leaders*. I'm not going to discuss the roles of others in the organization, although the goal is that everyone, up and down the chain of command, has a basic understanding of Lean and why it's important to the organization, so that they will willingly, if not zealously, participate in Lean improvement efforts.

Top Leaders

In the introduction to this book, Gary Kaplan, CEO of Virginia Mason, discussed the need for top leaders to commit thoroughly to Lean and to persevere in the face of resistance—to "drive home the message that Lean is the organization's management system." He also stressed the need for top leaders to lead by example (e.g., by participating in the improvement processes themselves and by being on the shop floor).

The need for top leadership commitment was reiterated in Chapter 1 by saying that the journey to becoming a world-class health organization is not for "the impatient or faint of heart." In particular, healthcare leaders must commit to *personally* leading the change effort. The first step is a change in *mind-set*. Healthcare leaders must believe that dramatic improvement is possible and be able to articulate a compelling picture of the future. Finally, healthcare leaders must clear their calendars and focus on Lean as the primary goal. This includes holding people's feet to the fire to ensure Lean is fully implemented.

Kaizen Promotion Office Leaders

Members of the KPO organization (see Chapter 5), whether in the KPO itself or a member of a *Kaizen* Operations Team (KOT) in one of the model service lines, are the CEO's Lean advance troops, so to speak. These people will work with line managers to help them understand how to implement Lean in their organizations and convey the importance of doing so. They are both Lean experts and, as the title of the organization suggests, Lean *promoters*. They also should be the CEO's eyes and ears as to how Lean implementation is proceeding. That means it's important to provide members of the KPO organization with an in-depth education on Lean early in the process.

Line Managers

Line managers, including physicians in managerial positions, also are expected to become Lean leaders over time, and as you'll see, every organization should have a training program to make sure they do. Initially, however, the most important thing is that line managers buy into the necessity for implementing Lean and be willing to follow the leads of top leadership and the KPO organization.

Bringing Non-Managerial Physicians on Board

In a healthcare system, there are no more important staff members than physicians. Gaining their buy-in to planned changes is essential. There's also no question that physicians occupy a different status in the healthcare industry than do typical employees of other industries. For one thing, many of them have their own practices and are linked to the medical system as much like individual contractors as employees. This offers physicians more autonomy within their organizations than members of other industries ordinarily enjoy. Persuasion, rather than directives, is the most effective means of achieving buy-in when dealing with physicians. Also, according to Mike Kaupa, COO of Park Nicollet, "Physicians are taught to be independent, to use their judgment, but their training in medical diagnoses and procedures is not consistent. So their professional model is not consistent with Lean's concept of standard work."

However, as Kaupa also points out:

Once clinicians understand that we're not standardizing their diagnostic services, they are much more favorable. One of the most powerful ways to convince physicians of the benefits of Lean is to take them to Japan. In fact, while I was there on my last visit, one of our physicians stood transfixed watching a Toyota mechanic perform his part of the auto-making process. After a while, he turned to me and said, "Look at that, Mike. Everything he's doing is value-added."

The approach Virginia Mason Medical Center took is instructive. Prior to beginning the Lean journey, physicians at Virginia Mason saw themselves as independent operators within a group practice. Changing their behavior to make it fit within an overall organizational change effort was not an easy sell. However, it would soon become clear that change had to occur if Virginia Mason was to survive.

In September of 2000, CEO Gary Kaplan organized an off-site retreat for all medical staff to discuss the current environment, including the need to become much more explicit regarding the obligations of the organization to its physicians and the obligations of Virginia Mason physicians to their organization. Following the retreat, Kaplan designated a committee of physicians to create a "physicians' compact." After a year, the compact was created and agreed upon. It outlines both organizational and individual physician responsibilities (see Appendix). The physicians' compact was soon followed by a similar compact between leaders and managers (Bohmer and Ferlins 2006).

While I stress the importance of bringing physicians on board, I don't want to exaggerate the difficulty of doing so, because physicians often become the most enthusiastic of Lean leaders.

Here's what Dr. Sam Carlson, CMO and executive vice president of Park Nicollet, has to say:

I first heard about Lean in 2002 at a Clinic Club meeting in Fargo, North Dakota, from a presentation made by Gary Kaplan and Mike Rona describing their early experience at Virginia

Mason. This was a new concept for me, but the potential to remove non–value-added work from healthcare, while improving quality and safety, was immediately appealing. I'm a firm believer that reducing unnecessary variation in our processes by developing and following standard work and measuring time will provide better quality and improve the patient's experience. We've discovered that where we thought we had standard work, we didn't. We were relying too much on memory and heroic efforts at the end process to provide safe care.

While Carlson admits there's been some physician resistance to change, he adds that "Most now understand that Lean is our improvement engine and there's something to gain by participating in it."

Common Requirements of All Lean Leaders

In addition to those qualities and skills I've already identified, all Lean leaders must:

- focus on the patient and on providing high-quality, waste- and defect-free healthcare;
- possess the political skill, the art, of finding the means to achieve the ends set forth in the vision;
- become active and willing participants and leaders in the Lean process; and
- possess the other skills common to good leaders (e.g., listening, delegating, setting priorities).

EDUCATING *KAIZEN* LEADERS

Being able to lead or manage the changes necessary to become a Lean organization requires an in-depth understanding of the Global Production System and Lean thinking. All those who will

Figure 6.1 Standard Certification Track for *Kaizen* Leaders

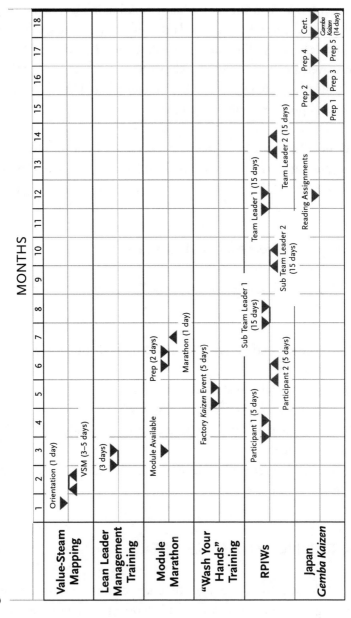

MONTHS

Value-Steam Mapping — Orientation (1 day), VSM (3–5 days)

Lean Leader Management Training — (3 days)

Module Marathon — Module Available, Prep (2 days), Marathon (1 day)

"Wash Your Hands" Training — Factory Kaizen Event (5 days)

RPIWs — Participant 1 (5 days), Participant 2 (5 days), Sub Team Leader 1 (15 days), Sub Team Leader 2 (15 days), Team Leader 1 (15 days), Team Leader 2 (15 days)

Japan *Gemba Kaizen* — Reading Assignments, Prep 1, Prep 2, Prep 3, Prep 4, Prep 5, Cert., *Gemba Kaizen* (14 days) be guiding the Lean journey must be educated about the principles, processes, methods, and tools involved—and *certified* as to their preparedness to be a *kaizen* leader. Experience has shown that 18 to 24 months is the minimum time necessary for this to occur.

Figure 6.1 shows in broad outline a typical certification track required for the success of Lean operations.

The sidebar on PNHS's certification process will give you a better idea of what's involved in creating Lean leaders. Please review this information and keep it in mind as I describe in more detail elements of the certification process.

The Park Nicollet Certification Process

Below is the actual timeline one group of leaders at PNHS followed to complete its certification process:

1. August 14, 2005: Reading materials, assignments, Lean modules, and quizzes.
2. Week of September 11, 2005: Value-stream map overview/orientation.
3. October 30–November 1, 2005: Management training (all groups together).
   - Global Production System overview
   - Toyota video
   - Quizzes (*Lean Thinking, Toyota Production System, A World Class Production System*)
   - Overview of 24 Lean modules
   - Teleconferences with experts
   - Batch vs. one-piece flow exercise
   - Beer game (a game focused on understanding *kanban*, inventory reduction, and flow)
4. Weeks of December 11, 2005; January 7, 2006; and January 14, 2006: Three-day intensive training.
5. Week of December 11: Groups 1–4, sessions 1 and 2.
   - Session 1, quizzes and module overviews (all 24)
   - Session 2, module overviews

(Continued on following page)

(Continued from previous page)

6. Week of January 7: Groups 1 and 2, module marathon. (The module marathon is exactly that, a marathon. It kicks off at 7:00 a.m. and continues without breaks until 5:00 p.m. Each participant must be prepared to present all 24 modules to a *takt* time of 10 minutes for each module. All are required to present the concept of standard operations [*takt* time, standard work in process, and standard work] and to explain the Lean House as described in Chapter 4. They are then asked to draw a name of another module and present it as well.)

7. Week of January 14: Groups 3 and 4, module marathon.

8. October 2006, and May 2007: "Wash Your Hands" *kaizen* training in Seattle, Washington.

9. June and November 2007 or June and November 2008: Trip to Japan for *gemba kaizen*. (Prior to the trip, those in certification are required to participate in two kaizen events, lead two sub-teams, and lead two teams.)
   • Three and one-half days of preparation (including reading four books, taking quizzes, and a full day of "cultural training")
   • 14 days in Japan

10. Six- and twelve-month reports after Japan trip: Follow-up reporting on progress made in mistake-proofing and work on value-stream maps.

11. Ongoing after Japan trip: Leaders are expected to participate as a team member in a *kaizen* event, lead another, and act as second in command of one more, as well as continue to lead everyday *kaizen* activities in their organization.

Selecting the Model Line and Value-Stream Mapping It

The Lean certification process normally starts with a group of about 30, led by the CEO, with team leaders and team sub-leaders appointed for each 10-person team. Their first job is to identify a key area to be the model line and collect data on it. Virginia Mason and Park Nicollet both started with surgery. It's important to begin with a model line closest to the patient rather than one in an upstream supporting service or with inventory.

The next step is to value-stream map the selected model line. Again, that means to pictorially represent the specific activities required to provide a patient service. Training, led by a *sensei,* is conducted on how to construct a value-stream map. The teams complete their value-stream maps and report out to each other, with the *sensei* critiquing the process. The teams are then issued their reading materials, about 60 days prior to the three-day management training.

The reading assignment may consist of these three books: *Lean Thinking* (second edition) by James P. Womack and Daniel T. Jones; *A World Class Production System* by John Black; and *Toyota Production System* by Taiichi Ohno.

Three-Day Management Training

Next, the group prepares to attend the three-day intensive training that includes taking a quiz on each book read and learn/do exercises involving 24 modules that encompass the Lean strategy and Lean tactics to transform the organization. At the three-day session, participants are furnished a CD-ROM containing these materials. In two months, participants will be required to present three of the modules to their fellow team members. Among the modules are these:

- Global Production System (Lean House) overview
- RPIW process (or *kaizen* event)
- Value-stream mapping
- 5S process
- Mistake-proofing
- *Kanban*
- Standard operations
- Continuous-flow production
- *Jidoka*
- Leveled production (*heijunka)*
- Multi-process operations

- Flow of materials and information
- Setup reduction
- Patient-Procedure/Quantity Analysis (PQA)
- Autonomous maintenance
- Visual controls *(andon)*
- Seven flows of medicine (see Chapters 1 and 7)
- World-class management system

Three-Day Intensive Training and Module Marathons

Participants are required to spend personal time studying and learning all modules related to Lean strategy and tactics, and, at the eight-hour module-marathon session, they draw the names of specific modules out of a hat to present to the other participants. No grade is assigned; participants either pass or fail. If a participant fails this exercise, he is given one more chance to present at a later date. A second failure is unacceptable regardless of one's position in the organization. The participant will not continue in the certification process. Also at the module marathon, participants are required to take a 45-page quiz on all the modules.

Next is the rigorous *event segment* in which those undergoing certification must be a participant, a sub-team leader, and a team leader in two *kaizen* events. These are planned out in a schedule and are conducted on the model line and led by the consultant. A considerable amount of time is required to complete this certification segment and no one is excused, regardless of position. For a participant, the time commitment is one week during the actual event. In addition to the week spent in the *kaizen* event, team leaders must also dedicate

- one full week three weeks prior to the beginning of the event,
- 50 percent of a week two weeks prior to the event, and
- 25 percent of the week immediately prior to the event.

This cycle is repeated twice.

"Wash Your Hands" *Kaizen* Event

Those in the certification process are next scheduled for a week-long "wash your hands" *kaizen* event—where participants observe and participate in an RPIW at Genie-Terex in Redmond, Washington. Genie-Terex has been implementing Lean for more than nine years.

A maximum of 45 participants are taken and organized into five teams, each with a team leader and team sub-leader under the guidance of a Japanese *sensei*. Participants spend Monday receiving preliminary training and then are bused to the factory to become familiar with the manufacturing process they will be work-

> **"Wash your hands" *kaizen* event:** Where participants in Lean education observe and participate in an RPIW on the factory floor

ing on. The following three days at Genie-Terex begin when the bus leaves the hotel at 6:00 a.m. On Friday, at the hotel, teams present their findings and learnings to the *senseis* and Genie-Terex factory managers in what is called a report-out. Each day, the team and team sub-leaders meet with the Japanese *sensei* to report progress and to receive a critique of their team's performance. Thursday evening is a late night as the teams prepare their detailed report-outs.

Japan Trip

Another requirement is that all Lean leaders in certification training must make the 14-day trip to Japan to practice *kaizen* on the factory floor (i.e., *gemba kaizen*). Preparation for the trip includes four days spread out over a sixty-day period, with required reading and quizzes and discussion about the many elements of TPS. Leaders also participate in a session conducted by Japanese trainers on Japanese culture and its dos and don'ts.

Once in Japan, participants spend a day at the Toyota Musuem of Industry and Technology learning about the evolution and history of TPS. The first Monday is devoted to training by Japanese *senseis.* The next two days, depending on whether it is a *gemba kaizen* or "super flow" trip, involve participating in *kaizen* efforts or sketching process flow at a Japanese company. The fourth day is a formal report of the results and learning.

The next step is visiting various world-class companies and Toyota suppliers to again study flow and sketch on the factory floor, with the final tour taking place at a Toyota factory. The training moves on to Tokyo and final debriefs and reports with finalization of action plans once back home. Both Virginia Mason and Park Nicollet are still engaged in taking leaders to Japan for training.

Following the Japan trip, leaders are expected to continue leading and participating in live *kaizen* events to improve their own operations.

> **Super flow:** Training in Japan where participants are taken to a variety of world-class manufacturing plants, including Toyota factories, to observe Lean in action and practice sketching the seven factory flows: people, information, equipment, raw materials, parts (subassemblies), final product, and engineering (gauges, tools, fixtures, and integration of all three)

DRIVING LEAN DEEP INTO THE ORGANIZATION

Besides the education of *kaizen* leaders, two other key steps are important for driving *kaizen* deep into your organization: 1) a Lean depth study (and related succession planning), and 2) a program to develop the next generation of leaders as *kaizen* masters (or a similar designation).

Lean Depth Study

The Lean depth study forces the organization's leaders to take a hard, objective look at the potential waste in the structure of the chain of command. Human resources should display detailed organization charts in a secure room. The organization charts should show all functions in the organization and the numbers of managers and other employees assigned to them, with all reporting relationships.

Lean depth study: A hard, objective look at the potential waste in the structure of the chain of command

The CEO assembles a small team that usually includes the COO, cheif financial officer (CFO), senior/executive vice presidents reporting to the CEO, the head of the KPO, and any other members of the CEO's decision-making team. My advice is to keep the group small.

The team's first job is to review all functions in terms of value-added and non–value-added, including non–value-added but required (usually because of a law or regulation). The next task is to review all managers in terms of the same value-added and non–value added criteria. Eliminate all non–value added functions and make a list of the managers judged to be non–value-added (those who the team believes will never support the transformation to Lean). Non–value-added managers who the team believes can be won over to Lean thinking should be given a trial period to get on board.

Two rules are important for success. The first is to take a vertical slice of the organization chart. Every management layer must have at least one non–value-added component removed. The second rule is the "7-7 rule." It requires that managers have at least seven managers reporting to them; otherwise they cannot be in management. Completion of the Lean depth study is essential to effective succession planning and the creation of replacement tables.

7-7 rule: The requirement that managers have at least seven managers reporting to them

Building *Kaizen* Masters

Once the organization has continuously implemented Lean for at least three years and has demonstrated the business discipline for long-term success, the next important step is to establish an executive-development program requiring all future leaders to acquire Lean mastery. The goal is to accelerate the management depth, commitment, knowledge, and passion for Lean, as well as its implementation, by further developing existing high-performing leaders.

CEO Gary Kaplan and then-president Mike Rona of Virginia Mason stepped up to the plate in 2003 and kicked off what they called the *Kaizen* Fellows educational program. By the end of 2008, this program will have graduated three groups of Fellows.

CEO David Wessner of Park Nicollet has adopted the same approach, with potential Lean leaders there identified as Leadership Fellows. Those selected to participate in late 2007 are high-performing leaders, role models, and experts in Lean who have completed Park Nicollet's rigorous 18-month certification process. The first group of participants are candidates already in high-level leadership positions. This first group is tasked with developing a course called *World Class Health Care* to be taught to all Park Nicollet employees. All Leadership Fellows will spend an additional four weeks of special training in Japan over a three-year period, to include participating in an international *kaizen* event.

In either case, some of the graduates will become members of the KPO, others will take new jobs, and some will maintain their current positions in the organization. As programs such as Park Nicollet's spread deeper into their organizations, they will include staff at lower levels of the organization who have been identified as top performers (e.g., clinicians, nurses, and other specialists).

These programs are similar to executive graduate-school programs in which participants are also expected to participate in evening and weekend classes. Such leadership-development programs are crucial to transforming any healthcare organization into one providing a world-class level of service.

OBSTACLES LEAN LEADERS MAY FACE

All Lean leaders need to learn how to overcome the roadblocks that organizations typically erect to protect themselves from change. In an October 24, 1991, speech to the American Production and Inventory Control Society, Bruce Gissing, the Boeing Commercial Airplane Group's executive vice president for operations, identified some of these obstacles. Table 6.1 details Gissing's list of obstacles, along with my thoughts on some potential solutions.

Table 6.1 Obstacles to Lean and Their Potential Solutions

Obstacle	Description	Solution
Vocabulary	This is particularly true in the use of the word "program." This word use suggests a temporary activity and implies that quality efforts are short-term solutions or quick fixes to problems. Even worse, a quality "program" is usually interpreted by employees as *separate* from a company's line of business.	Make Lean the way of life for the organization. (Both the Virginia Mason Production System and the Park Nicollet Management System use the same Lean House. So do many other companies implementing the pure Japanese model.)
Management Inertia	Often it takes a crisis to create the proper climate for improvement efforts.	If you don't currently have a crisis, create one.
Size	The larger an organization, the more difficult to improve its processes.	Start small and focused by driving a "mile deep and an inch wide" in establishing model lines (i.e., focus on individual parts of an organization initially, implement Lean as fully as possible, and make these model lines "building blocks" for the entire system).
Cold Feet	The greatest perceived peril is that a change in the process won't work and that this will cause the production line to stop.	Get the right *senseis* to focus the organization on a model line and demonstrate the power of Lean.
Full Plate	People often claim to be too busy to take on a change effort	Lean forces a paradigm shift in how everyday work is to be done.

(Continued on following page)

Obstacle	Description	Solution
The White-Collar Challenge	Some believe that white-collar work is unique to the individual worker and can't be measured or standardized, or fear that the quality-improvement efforts will eliminate jobs.	Include in the overall organization's KPO a corporate KOT that tackles white-collar waste. Additionally, emphasize that improvement efforts can enable the organization to increase patient throughput, thus maintaining overall jobs.
Impatience	People may want to drop the improvement effort if results aren't immediate.	Start *kaizen* immediately and get immediate results.
Low-Hanging Fruit	That is, picking off the easiest improvement opportunities first. This is a possible solution to the *impatience* obstacle, but it is a danger as well. People may grow discouraged with the larger challenges if the smaller ones can be conquered too easily.	Resource your improvement effort with a good mix of sprinters and long-distance runners. (Toyota says, "Good thinking means good products.")
Sacred Cows	These are practices and beliefs considered off-limits to questioning.	Make it clear from the start that "We will kill all sacred cows."
Loss of Executive Focus	A corporate crisis can distract the top leaders.	A corporate crisis is exactly what will promote Lean's implementation and success. However, once leadership has analyzed the crisis, it should assign a senior executive to resolve it, if possible, leaving top leaders to focus on implementing Lean. If the crisis affects the overall operations of the company, the leadership should use the crisis to emphasize the need for increased commitment to Lean and accelerated improvement efforts.
Fear of Change	Historically, employees find change to be unpleasant and anxiety producing.	Communicate, communicate, communicate, and continually publicize successes.
Too Many Cooks (or Recipes)	Failing to focus on one, correct improvement path for one's organization.	As Dr. Joseph Juran said, the CEO must communicate "proof of need," set the path for the organization, and keep the organization on track.

Maintaining a Long-Range View

Keep in mind that the Lean journey is a 20-year strategy with four five-year time blocks (see Figure 5.4). You must field a top-to-bottom, highly competent organizational leadership team that will, by the end of the first five years, be in place and capable of carrying the improvement process forward. This is a challenge. At the present time, the only healthcare organizations anywhere in the world that I know of that have fully committed to this total strategy are Virginia Mason Medical Center and Park Nicollet Health Services.

Will your organization meet the challenge and join them?

CHAPTER TAKEAWAYS

- Members of the KPO and KOTs are the CEO's Lean advance troops.
- However, line managers also are expected to become Lean leaders over time.
- Lean leaders must focus on the patient, possess political skills, get involved in Lean activities, and possess the other skills common to good leaders.
- A healthcare system implementing Lean should put in place a Lean leader certification program to create Lean leaders. This will require 18 to 24 months and a trip to Japan.
- Leaders must identify non–value-added activities and the people assigned to them. Non–value-added activities must be eliminated. The people assigned to them should be reassigned to value-added activities, if possible, but only *if* they are supportive of Lean.
- Leaders may face obstacles, but there are solutions.

REFERENCES

Bohmer, R.M.J., and E.M. Ferlins. 2006. "Virginia Mason Medical Center." *Harvard Business Review* September 7.

Gissing, B. 1991. "The Road to World-Class Competitiveness." Speech to the American Productivity and Inventory Control Society, Seattle, October 24.

CHAPTER 7

Flow in a Healthcare Environment

OVERVIEW: In this chapter, you'll examine the concept of *flow* in the Lean healthcare system—specifically, the seven critical flows of healthcare. Each flow is explained, with examples given of ways to improve performance. Helpful questions should stimulate the reader to think of ways to improve performance in each of these flows in their own healthcare system.

THE SEVEN CRITICAL HEALTHCARE FLOWS

Flow is a key concept in a Lean system. As with the human body, when a healthcare system is healthy and operates at peak performance, everything flows. And, as with the human body, when flow is obstructed or misdirected, problems occur. As mentioned in Chapter 1, there are seven critical flows essential to the healthy operation of a healthcare system. These are:

1. Flow of patients
2. Flow of clinicians
3. Flow of medication
4. Flow of supplies

5. Flow of information
6. Flow of equipment
7. Flow of process engineering

A healthcare leader should view these flows as targeted areas for improvement.

Case Example 1—Using the Seven Flows to Improve Performance

The Park Nicollet cancer care center used the seven flows as areas to target for rapid improvement. This table illustrates the flow and the improvement target.

Flow Area	Improvement Target
Patient Flow	Provide patients with one location for all needs. Reduce patient travel and movement by 50 percent.
Clinician Flow	Reduce clinicians' travel by 30 percent at one site so they can be more attentive to patients' needs.
Medication Flow	Reduce inventory and number of storage locations by 50 percent. This results in significant reduction in movement.
Supply Flow	Reduce storage locations and inventory by 50 percent, and greatly reduce movement of supplies.
Information Flow	Rely less on electronic information and more on personal contact with patients.
Equipment Flow	Use 25 percent less equipment for the same volume of patients.
Flow of Process Engineering	Reduce number of instruments used by 25 percent for the same volume of patients by eliminating duplication and minimizing movement of instruments.

This chapter will look at each of the seven flows, how they appear in healthcare environments, and the negative impact when each flow is stopped or slowed.

Flow of Patients

The flow of patients through a medical center should be natural, quick, and simple. This relieves stress on the patient, the patient's family, and the healthcare staff. Patients have time demands besides medical treatment; they want their time to be managed wisely in the medical facility and they become impatient when they have to wait needlessly or feel their time is not being respected or honored.

Observe a patient's journey through the system to receive primary-care treatment and you may see a path through patient registration, to a nursing station, to the doctor's office, and then possibly to radiology or to the lab. The patient may then return to the doctor's office or go to the pharmacy before exiting. How can that path or process be streamlined?

Case Example 2—Patient Flow

At Virginia Mason Medical Center, the cancer center team reduced the walking distance for chemotherapy patients. Prior to the *kaizen* event, the team discovered that the floor plan required some of the sickest patients to walk up to 748 feet. After the improvement, which brought the services directly to the patient instead of expecting the patient to walk to receive many different services, overall patient travel was reduced to 181 feet.

Another *kaizen* event focused on patient flow in the emergency department. When the admission process was moved to the patient's bedside, patient flow was streamlined, thus ensuring quicker treatment and eliminating long waits and delays for the patient.

A good way to analyze patient flow is via a standard work sheet as described in Chapter 4. This helps establish the baseline, distance, and improvement opportunities in eliminating steps that do not add value to the patient's care. Use a stopwatch to time patient flow.

Figure 7.1 shows the route a patient travels at Virginia Mason's new Center for Hyperbaric Medicine (see Chapter 10). The patient enters the center at lower left and makes her way to the hyperbaric chamber (the large structure at far right) via a number of stops, including reception, changing room, examination room, etc. By using a standard work sheet in this way, one can determine whether patient flow is as efficient as possible.

Here are some ways to improve patient flow:

- *Minimize patient walking; bring the services to the patient.* This is exactly what happens when an ambulance is sent out. Not only is the service brought to the patient, but all the materials and supplies needed are at the point of use in a very organized fashion.
- *Create flexible spaces that can be reconfigured based on the patient and the procedure.* Make your cells (work areas) open so patients and staff can move easily from one to another, improving flow and balance. This openness makes backlogs in the system much more apparent.
- *Eliminate schedulers/planners.* When the process follows a consistent and repeatable flow, extra people are not needed to ensure the process is adhered to. Patients are treated on a first-in/first-out basis.
- *Stop the process when problems occur (*jidoka*).* Stopping the process when problems occur, as Virginia Mason does with its Patient Safety Alerts, may slow patient flow initially. However, flow will speed up in the long run as *jidoka* allows patient health and safety problems to be addressed as soon as they occur rather than passing them along or allowing them to multiply.

Figure 7.1 Standard Work Sheet of Patient Flow at Virginia Mason's Center for Hyperbaric Medicine

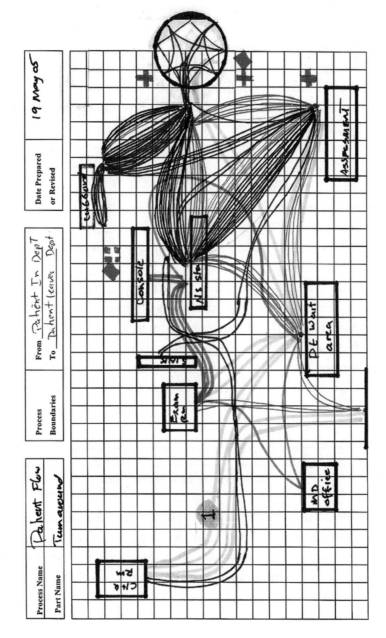

Source: Virginia Mason Medical Center. Used with permission.

Pokayoke: The Japanese term for a mistake-proofing device or procedure to prevent defects

- *Apply quality checks at each step of the process. Pokayoke* is the Japanese term for a mistake-proofing device or procedure to prevent defects (e.g., a "screen" for order input that identifies orders falling outside the normal pattern). Healthcare practitioners are very intelligent. They should be empowered to conduct quality checks at each process step and to stop the process if patient safety or confidentiality is being violated.

- *Use between-process time productively.* Be creative. Provide patient education via in-house materials or video, schedule follow-up visits, coordinate with other clinicians, and devise easy methods to obtain medications. Countless actions can be taken to optimize between-process times.

- *Implement sequential order of processing.* Study your patient processes and flows. Put the patient's process steps in sequential order to eliminate the need for rework or backtracking of patient steps.

- *Double up.* Try to schedule as many patient services as possible for the same visit (e.g., scheduling lab testing or radiology in concert with the doctor's appointment).

- *Use one-piece flow to keep patients on a first-in, first-out (FIFO) system.* Handle each patient one at a time, addressing all his needs.

- *Understand and proceed according to* takt *time* (as explained in Chapter 4).

Case Example 3—Patient Flow

At Park Nicollet, RPIW teams targeted standard rooming procedures as a method to eliminate variation. Prior to the implementation of standard rooming, clinical information gathered during the patient rooming process (weight, blood pressure, heart

---

rate, allergies, and a review of the patient's medications) varied significantly. When this clinical information is not consistently collected, it increases the possibility of defects and patient errors.

With standard rooming, each patient has the same clinical information gathered and reviewed—every time, at every visit, with only a few items designated PRN (as needed). Examples of PRN include temperature (if infection is suspected) and height (required only once a year). Otherwise, patients can always expect to have their weight, blood pressure, heart rate, allergies, and medication reviewed.

Questions to consider regarding patient flow:

- Which areas in your facility experience prolonged wait time?
- When and where are clinicians waiting for patient arrival?
- Where are the opportunities to optimize flow?
- If you discover unavoidable between-process time, can you build in methods to address educational or scheduling needs, or order medications for the patient?
- Can you bring the service closer to the patient (e.g., can lab work be performed near the patient rather than sending the patient to a central lab?)
- How much time per patient is allotted? Is this time too little or too much, based on the patient load and the severity of cases?

Flow of Clinicians

Healthcare clinicians are the people most instrumental in providing value-added work to health-system processes. The flow of clinicians between the clinic, the hospital, and other patient-care delivery centers should be quick, easy, and stress-free for both clinicians and patients. Doctors, nurses, and other practitioners forced to scramble around, traveling from one appointment to another, are often stressed. This sometimes results in a curt demeanor and poor patient relations. (Studies show that physicians known for a good bedside manner and for taking time to know their patients are less likely to be sued for malpractice.)

Case Example 4—Flow of Clinicians

At Virginia Mason, the clinician in the gastrointestinal (GI) department was scheduling post-procedure patients for consults on the same day that procedures were scheduled. This took him away from the GI lab, down into his examination area, and caused delays for the patients and other clinicians in the GI procedural area. To improve this situation, the GI team created a post-procedure card that enabled clinicians to indicate if the patients needed to be seen by the clinician or could be discharged from the recovery room by the RN.

Another doctor was batching his dictations at the end of the day, extending his day and making his task more difficult, as he had to recall patient information long after the procedure was completed. To improve this situation, the clinician agreed to *standard work* where he dictated his notes immediately after a procedure, before the next patient arrived. Prior to this improvement, there were about nine batched dictations at the end of the day; after this improvement, there were none.

Here are some ways you can improve your flow of clinicians:

- *Cross-train employees.* Speed the flow of people through the system. If cross-training is made available, an employee in one area can float into another area and perform the job if someone is absent. For example, a cross-trained nursing assistant in the internal medicine department may be asked to float into the obstetrics/gynecology department.

- *Understand* takt *time and cycle time.* Know how much time is assigned to each step in your unit's process to help level the workload (*heijunka*) and staff it appropriately. If a cardiac-care unit normally handles 20 patients in a day and only 10 beds are full, determine where else in the medical center the clinicians are needed.

- *Examine the motion of hands, feet, and eyes as staff members work in an area.* Eliminate wasted motion by providing sequential, standard work. Motions should not be repetitive. Process steps should follow one another and fall into a logical sequence.

- *Design work areas with ergonomics in mind.* Strive to eliminate bending, heavy lifting, or twisting. Is everything within strike distance (the distance between the waist and shoulders, and within a 45-degree angle to the right and to the left of the clinician)? Ergonomically designed work stations benefit the worker and the medical center. First, they prevent injuries and lost workdays and make it easier for clinicians to do their jobs and optimize their time. Second, they help protect the organization from workers' compensation claims. Creating ergonomic work environments sends the message that the organization cares about its employees.

- *Make operations one-touch wherever possible to avoid duplicative effort, and do not tolerate rework!* Action within a process should take place only once. Empower every clinician to conduct quality checks to ensure that work is eliminated and defects detected and removed. Progress can be achieved over time through *kaizen* events (RPIWs).

- *Eliminate stationary objects, such as chairs or stools, wherever possible.* Fit any necessary, stationary pieces with wheels so they can be pushed aside if they're obstructing clinician flow. Standing promotes easy movement from station to station.

- *Avoid unreasonableness (*muri*).* Plan every step and action to optimize employee movement and minimize patient travel.

There should be *no wasted motion*. Simplify any process by studying it and determining the best practice and the best sequence of actions.

- *Place all supplies, instruments, and materials as close to the clinician as possible.* Set up a crash cart, for example, so that medical personnel can immediately respond to a code. Another example: create a tray prepared for surgery or a cart prepared for an IV nurse on which everything needed is within reach and at shoulder-to-waist level. Replenish these carts and trays at night or between shifts.

Case Example 5—Flow of Clinicians

The administrative workload for nurses at Park Nicollet's family medicine department was growing. Each clinician took a different approach to his work. Doctors were coming in early to dictate, starting appointments late, seeing patients over lunch, and staying after hours to complete their work. The overflow work included telephone messages, dictations, transcription, medication refills, laboratory results reviews, and patient letters. Initial data showed, on average, clinicians were spending an additional two to three hours each day handling these tasks. Parallel to this, nursing support staff were in a similar situation with additional duties, including constant paperwork, faxing, photocopying, chart labeling, etc.

The department conducted a *kaizen* event focused on leveling the workload of the staff (clinicians, nursing support staff, and the department assistant). The deliverable from the workshop was that each healthcare practitioner should focus exclusively on what was needed from her specific role. For example, the clinician's duties were reduced to seeing the patient, completing a charge ticket, dictating notes, and performing one to two small tasks (such as signing off on a prescription or reviewing a lab result).

Prior to the *kaizen* event, one of the doctors was seeing, on average, 17.5 patients in a 12-hour work day, or about 1.5 patients an hour. By the end of the *kaizen* event week, he was seeing 22 patients in a workday of just over 11 hours, a 30 percent increase in productivity. He had fewer dictations left at the end of the day because he was completing them after each patient visit (one-piece flow). He also experienced a 71 percent reduction in phone messages.

Some questions to consider regarding clinician flow:

- What is the average length of time required to process and treat one patient?
- How many patients does your unit treat in a day? In a week?
- Where can you better arrange work cells? How easy would it be to reconfigure the work space?
- Is it possible to set up satellite labs or pharmacies for smaller, less invasive treatments, reducing the time a patient or a clinician spends traveling to a central site? (If it's easy for a patient to obtain medicines from a pharmacy at the treatment site, you save the patient time and you obtain the funds from selling the pharmaceuticals.)

Flow of Medication

The flow of medication through the system supports the flow of patients. Optimally, medications flow through the system on a just-in-time basis—that is, the correct medication in the amount needed, where it is needed, when it is needed. Here are some ways to improve medication flow:

- *Provide one-piece flow with signal/pull from clinician.* Locate medications as close as possible to the point of use.

- *Combine (kit) medications commonly used together in one container where possible.* Add to the kits any additional medications prescribed by the physician. Re-kitting medications the night before discharge enables a patient and family to exit the system more quickly. Waiting for pharmaceuticals is annoying to the patient, if not anxiety provoking, and can tie up a hospital bed.

Case Example 6—Flow of Medication

Virginia Mason maintained a zero avoidable–drug event goal. The successful implementation of computerized physician order entry (CPOE) resulted in decreases in the number of errors in ordering medication. This process eliminated the doctors' handwritten orders, historically fraught with the potential for errors.

- *Create smaller, specialized satellite pharmacies where possible.* Satellite pharmacies bring pharmacy staff closer to high–patient population locations and make it easier to eliminate backlogs and long queues.
- *Introduce point of use.* Be creative. How can point-of-use storage be applied so that patients obtain the meds they need, with no waiting, at a reasonable price?

> **Point of use:** Where medication storage is located where the patient is treated

For example, what if you created a pharmacy cart designed for the pharmacist to make point-of-use deliveries at the end of the day based on a *kanban* system? (A *kanban* system can signal when to restock supplies on a prudent, JIT basis; see Chapter 8.)
- *Make pharmaceutical samples available in the doctor's office so patients can try the medication for a week and see how it affects them.* Along with the samples, provide a prescription for the medication. If the samples work for a patient, she can take the prescription to a local pharmacy and get it filled.

- *Conduct patient-discharge planning the night before dismissal.* Write orders and prepare medications to send with the patient upon departure. Some hospitals have a "will call" window on the first floor near the parking garage so patients can pick up medications as they leave.

Case Example 7—Flow of Medication

The cost of medications is one of the highest care expenses at Park Nicollet. Controlling this cost and managing the related inventory is crucial to the financial well-being of the facility, so the improvement team introduced *kanban* to the medication inventory.

In three departments at one clinic site, approximately 628 different medications with a price tag of $32,513 were kept in inventory. Of these, 28 percent were high-cost, low-use medications—items regularly stocked but used infrequently. Also, the pharmacy receiving and distributing the medications was having a difficult time deciphering the prescriptions and tracking down the right people and departments doing the ordering.

Through two *kaizen* events, *kanban* was implemented in family medicine, internal medicine, pediatrics, and, eventually, urgent care. Doing so reduced inventory by 29 percent overall and reduced cost by 50 percent. Additionally, the surplus items from the three departments were accepted back by suppliers for a one-time credit of just under $20,000.

Aside from cost and space, *kanban* saved three hours of ordering and another three hours of restocking these medications each week. Previously, one person was pulled off the floor once a week for a total of six hours to do this work. Pictorial standard work was developed and implemented, reducing ordering and restocking to just a few minutes for each department. The pharmacy, by instituting standard work and the use

(Continued on following page)

(Continued from previous page)

of one common ordering fax, has maintained a zero incorrect order rate for these four departments.

Questions to consider regarding medication flow:

- Can a satellite pharmacy be placed at each service delivery center so that medications are delivered quickly and effectively?
- Where can you pre-kit medications and stimulate flow? Can medications be kitted the night before patients are to be discharged?
- How often are medications being ordered?
- Are you stocking medications you don't use regularly (just in case)? Are some of them reaching their expirations dates before use? Are you increasing costs by being overly cautious?

Flow of Supplies

Supplies support the healthcare team in its delivery of quality patient care. The quick and easy flow of supplies ensures that the right supplies are delivered to the right area in the right amount.

Case Example 8—Flow of Supplies

At Virginia Mason, the operating room staff has been continually standardizing the case procedure cards by which they request supplies and instruments from central services. This work has decreased the delivery of unused supplies and ensures that what is needed is delivered JIT, reducing the need for inventory and storage.

Most units in the medical center have a *kanban* system in place for the replenishment of supplies, eliminating the need for staff to manually count inventory.

Here are some ways to improve supply flow:

- *Create systems where the supplies flow directly to point of use.*
  Study the most common patterns of the supply chain and
  distribution on a daily, weekly, and monthly basis. This will
  provide the data to determine your greatest leverage points.
- *Deliver supplies on a JIT basis.* Make sure the only material on
  hand is the minimum prudence dictates and that it can be
  replenished quickly. *Kanban* provides an effective process. For
  example, a 2-bin *kanban* enables a unit to have the materials it
  needs when needed, and to signal central supply for restocking
  when only one bin is left. The empty bin is sent to central supply to be restocked and delivered back to the unit. The bins
  should be labeled and/or color-coded to make sure the right
  bin returns to the right unit. As the medical center uses *kanban*
  more and more in all aspects of service and patient care, the
  healthcare system will move to a total pull system—even more
  so if suppliers are included in the *kanban* system.
- *Plan how to present material and sequence its use.* Material
  should be stocked and supplied according to a FIFO method.
  For example, if the hospital has nine operating rooms (ORs),
  central supply should know the schedule of operations per
  room per surgeon. Then it can kit the sterilized OR packets
  so each operating room can pull a packet for each patient and
  procedure.
- *Make the flow visual for simple control.* "Make it visual" (or
  sweep) is one of the elements in a 5S process. This means
  devising visual controls, such as differently colored labels, bulletin boards, and signs, that enable clinicians and staff within
  the area to see how the flow is going.

Questions to consider regarding supply flow:

- How can you create systems to bring supplies into the
  medical center in a quick and efficient way? Is there pull

from patient service delivery centers to central supply and out to suppliers?

- Where can you *make it visual* so that patients or employees can scan at a glance and tell what is happening and what action to take next?
- Is safety stock necessary? If so, where?

Case Example 9—Flow of Supplies

At Park Nicollet, medical supplies were numerous and expensive, and departmental needs varied. Supplies were usually ordered in large batches. Excess supplies were stacked in supply closets, cupboards, drawers, and other spaces. With the implementation of *kanban*, the management of supplies became much simpler.

All supplies were moved to one common storage space. Bins were set up with *kanban* cards. When some items were more difficult to obtain, safety stock (an additional amount) was provided. Inventory staff used a cart to stock supplies and then distributed them to each exam room.

This decreased the stocking rooms and made ordering easier. When supplies dwindled to the minimum amount required, the *kanban* card was pulled and the item ordered to maintain prudent levels. Looking for secret stashes of items (that may have expired) was eliminated.

The storage of linens was also improved. While not on a *kanban* system, pictures of the linens were placed on the shelves to assign location and the shelves were set at a specific height. When the linen delivery staff put the linen on the shelf and stacked it to the top of the shelf, the right amount was in place every time, without manual counting.

Flow of Information

The efficient and effective flow of information enables timely patient care, a high quality of care, and enhanced safety. You don't want a break in information flow—for example, a missing chart or lab results—to interrupt patient flow. Neither do you want incorrect or missing information (e.g., allergies to medications) to endanger the patient. Consider how many times hospital clinicians take time to verify patient identification. This is a quality check to ensure that the correct person receives the correct treatment.

Value-stream mapping can tell you how information flows through the system and where redundancy and rework exist. It can tell you how many data systems exist that all ask the same questions and keep the same data.

Case Example 10—Flow of Information

At Virginia Mason, patients checking in were asked to inspect the computer screen for errors in their information, ensuring accuracy and timeliness. Thus, mistakes were discovered and corrected immediately, ensuring the correct billing and emergency contact information.

In the Virginia Mason patient-discharge process, patients are given a sheet that informs them of the goals they must reach in order to go home (e.g., can you walk, eat, not be in pain). This sheet is posted in the room and the patient is asked to keep track of his progress. Thus, discharge planning is communicated in a visual way among the care team, the patients, and their families.

Here are some ways to stimulate the flow of information:

- *Have information travel with the patient.* Patients can bring their files with them to the next clinician they see. Provide patients' x-rays on CD-ROM as they proceed to the next specialist.

- *Use only the minimum information necessary to provide the specific service.* Healthcare institutions are required by law to keep medical records for seven years. But does the entire volume of information, or only the most recent and relevant exams, have to travel with the patient? For example, medical insurance cards often provide all necessary information to quickly enter a patient into the system.

- *Make patient information portable.* Can you electronically upload a patient's medical history to a memory stick (a small, portable memory-storage device often called a "thumb drive") and periodically update it? Can you give a copy to patients to take with them?

- *Determine how information will flow when designing a process.* Where should information be visual? Where should it travel electronically? When should the patient carry a hard copy? Where should the information be stored and how will it be retrieved?

- *Implement open-room arrangements that facilitate the flow of information between clinicians and make transferring information at nursing shift change easy.* Making patient status easily visible on a whiteboard can provide all the information needed. The two shifts may only need to check that they agree on the meaning of all terms and procedures.

Case Example 11—Flow of Information

To comply with the requirements for clinician orders of the Joint Commission, a non-profit national healthcare accrediting body, Park Nicollet staff determined that a standardized clinician-order form was necessary, as well as a standard process for completing the form. These standards affected both nursing and clinician staff.

The "fuchsia form" (a visual cue, named for the fuchsia-colored stripe on the bottom of the form) was developed as a quick tool

---

for both nursing support and clinician staff. Staff checks off boxes indicating whether standard preventive services have been performed (e.g., laboratory testing for cholesterol; immunizations for influenza or other illnesses; and health-maintenance services, such as mammograms).

Questions to consider regarding information flow:

- Where and how can you make information travel with the patient?
- Are you providing information clinicians don't use?
- Where do you find redundancy and rework in information flow?
- Can we put all the vital patient information on an electronic card that can simply be swiped upon arrival at the medical center?
- What is your process for flow of information? How can you improve this flow to better serve your patients?

Flow of Equipment

Medical equipment must be available and readily accessible when needed. Long queues to obtain treatment may indicate the need for additional equipment. Make sure a preventive maintenance schedule is in place to avert machinery breakdowns or unplanned repairs.

Case Example 12—Flow of Equipment

At Virginia Mason, medical equipment was stored in a centralized equipment room and moved where it was needed when it was needed. Staff conducted a *kaizen* event and decided to move the equipment closer to the treatment-delivery site. This eliminated the need to search for equipment and ensured that the equipment was ready for use when and where needed.

- *Apply* jidoka *to determine when to use a people solution or an equipment solution.* In our technological age, it's particularly easy to buy costly devices that don't actually improve patient care or medical system efficiency as advertised. Carefully analyze whether any activity is most efficiently performed by a machine or a person.
- *Arrange equipment in a sequence that facilitates one-piece flow of patients, clinicians, and information.* Wherever possible, avoid locating equipment where it adds extra travel time for patients or staff.
- *Whenever possible, use right-sized, small, homemade economical equipment on wheels that's easy to move and light enough for one person to manage.* This limits walls and monuments (immovable equipment or furnishings) so the space available can be configured in the most effective and efficient way possible.
- *Optimize equipment use.* Machines can operate 24 hours a day, seven days a week. Are you optimizing the use of yours, for example, by offering MRI services in two or three shifts?
- *Be flexible in your equipment use.* Explore adding or subtracting equipment as demand varies. Can equipment easily be dismantled or folded up and stored close by if it is not currently needed (but will be necessary in the future)?

Monument: Immovable piece of equipment or furnishing

Case Example 13—Flow of Equipment

The Park Nicollet diabetic care center introduced the extended lab menu (ELM) in the summer of 2006 to help improve next-visit setup for diabetes patients. With ELM, the staff provides blood-testing equipment onsite for a 30-minute turnaround time, with lab results available at the time of the patient's appointment. Prior to ELM, patients had lab tests taken after the visit, which were sent offsite for processing, and all results were batched. The patient-notification process included both telephone calls and mailings. These processes were fraught with rework and defects, as well as being time consuming and costly.

Four sites trialed and implemented the ELM process. Patient satisfaction with ELM is 100 percent positive. The next step is to see where, beyond diabetes, ELM can be used.

Questions to consider regarding flow of equipment:

- How will a piece of equipment improve patient flow, quality of care, and safety? Is it the most cost-efficient solution?
- How often will the equipment be used? Can it be used more if demand increases?
- Is the equipment located where it makes the most sense in terms of patient flow? Can it easily be moved to the point of service delivery?
- Does every piece of equipment have a preventive-maintenance schedule? Is it being followed?

Flow of Process Engineering

For the most part, the process engineers in a healthcare system are *clinicians* who lead and participate in *kaizen* activities, perhaps members of an RPIW or a KOT. Consequently, process-engineering flow can be defined as the footprints and traces that clinicians create and leave in the medical center as they focus on synchronizing all of the other six flows of medicine in their daily work and in improvement activities.

Case Example 14—Flow of Process Engineering

Virginia Mason maintains a center for hyperbaric medicine. Standard work was developed for all roles in the center. The standard work for all clinicians is printed on laminated pocket-sized

(Continued on following page)

(Continued from previous page)

cards. They clearly define all required tasks, who's responsible for performing the tasks, and the time it should take to complete each task. The standard work cards are located near the time clock, making it easy for each employee to grab her card and begin work upon arrival.

Some facts about process engineering:

- *Process engineering is judged by the simplicity of the work process.* The simpler it is, the easier to document, to cross-train, and to remain open to change.
- *Process engineering should use simple instruments and measurements versus complex and costly ones.* Enough said.
- *Improvement efforts are driven by* takt *time.* The process engineer can help other clinicians calculate *takt* time for their processes and patient services.
- *The process engineer must stay with the new process until* takt *time and quality are met on the floor for three weeks (according to our Japanese senseis).* The goal is to have the process become part of the routine, as well as to eliminate any implementation difficulties. If the process engineer does not stay with the new process, it's easy to slip back into the old way of doing things.
- *Process flow determines the profits of the company.* With improved flow, the healthcare system will find costs decreasing and the quality of patient care improving. This is the beauty of a Lean environment. It's a more pleasant work environment that increases quality and patient safety, while also being less expensive and more profitable.

Case Example 15—Tracking the Seven Flows Within a Medical Center

Virginia Mason was planning how to structure its physical plant for the year 2015. Staff tracked the current status of all seven healthcare flows through their facility. The process engineer created a three-dimensional mock-up of the facility, and each of the flows was identified with a different color of yarn. The yarn was laid out on a board to demonstrate how the flow actually occurs at the facility. Four major high-volume patient portals into the facility were identified.

With this model, an improvement team identified the waste imbedded in the current flows. The mock-up also provided a hands-on way to identify bottlenecks in the space available and points where multiple handoffs were occurring. This three-dimensional model helped the team identify the tremendous amount of waste for both patients and clinicians in the current healthcare flows, along with the misuse of equipment, supplies, and medication. Through this modeling process, the team was able to develop a new model for the future, one that would reduce waste and eliminate errors.

Questions to consider regarding the flow of process engineering:

- Are your processes enhancing or interfering with efficient functioning of any of the other six flows of healthcare?
- Is the work process you're following/implementing simple and effective? Will it likely decrease or increase the chance of mistakes or defects?
- Are the instruments and measurements you're using easy to use and cost effective?
- Are you basing your processes on *takt* time?

SUMMARY

Studying the seven flows in your facility and identifying the waste within the processes can lead to creative ways of improving both the facility and patient care. Improved flow creates greater patient satisfaction and greater staff satisfaction. It also reduces the chance for errors and increases the percentage of value-added work. If you want to improve flow, go to the place of action and see what the clinicians are doing. Look for long wait times or clutter piling up in the system.

Takt time is a crucial measure of the seven flows in your medical center. It is the primary tool to measure demand for the medical center's rooms, equipment, and patient delivery services.

The seven flows work together and complement each other. An existing facility can be redesigned to enhance and streamline all those flows. The seven flows also can—and should— be applied in the preliminary design of a new facility or site. This will optimize the new design and improve all seven flows of healthcare.

Kaizen is everybody's responsibility in the medical center.

CHAPTER TAKEAWAYS

- When a healthcare system is healthy and operating at peak performance, everything flows.
- There are seven flows critical to the healthy operation of a healthcare system: patients, clinicians, medication, supplies, information, equipment, and process engineering.
- These flows work together and complement each other to produce *takt* time (service delivered at the rate of demand).
- Continuous incremental improvement (*kaizen*) is everybody's responsibility.

CHAPTER 8

Kanban and the Supply Chain

OVERVIEW: This chapter examines *kanban* and the supply chain. What is *kanban*? Why is it important? How does it relate to other concepts we've learned, such as just in time, *heijunka*, and *takt* time? We'll look at examples of various applications of *kanban* in the healthcare setting, including the 2-bin system, and the benefits of using *kanban*. Along the way, we'll hear from those responsible for implementing *kanban* and learn their experiences.

WHAT IS *KANBAN*?

Previous chapters have mentioned and given brief examples of the use of *kanban*, which we've defined as a way of automatically signaling when new parts, supplies, or services are needed. More examples are provided in this chapter and in chapters ahead.

Kanban is entirely consistent with, and dependent upon, the concept of pull production. In the case of healthcare, the demand of the patient or the clinician causes a service or supply item to be provided. Two examples follow.

- At Virginia Mason's Center for Hyperbaric Medicine, *kanban* cards are used both to identify and pull the patient along the treatment path. The patient places a large *kanban* card in a plastic holder at each point of service (e.g., changing room, exam room, hyperbaric chamber). This card notifies the provider that the patient has arrived and needs some type of treatment or procedure. In this way, the patient can proceed at an individual pace, with the *kanban* cards signaling to the providers the action required of them. (More detail is provided in the case study of the center in the Chapter 10.)
- Another simple example from Virginia Mason's hyperbaric center is the way it restocks its tongue depressors. The person responsible for supplies places 20 tongue depressors in a clearly labeled jar, with 10 of them bundled together with a rubber band. When the first 10 are gone and it becomes necessary to remove the rubber band, a *kanban* card is sent to central supply requesting 10 more tongue depressors.

GENERIC BENEFITS OF A *KANBAN* SYSTEM

Why is *kanban* important? Because, according to Katsuya Koide and Takeshi Iwata (2006), it's "an essential tool for implementing a just-in-time production process." And JIT production is the key to driving waste from one's system.

A clear and simple statement of the benefits a *kanban* system can provide is given by Koide and Iwata in their paper "Deployment of a Global *Kanban* System":

> The *kanban* system provides a superior tool for production control, visual management, and *kaizen*. As a visual management tool, a *kanban* indicates mainly 1) production priority, 2) production status, and 3) in-process inventory (preventing over- and under-production). The *kanban* system also provides an excellent mechanism for identifying

problems in both process and products quickly, and can help determine problem-solving priorities for remedial action. The *kanban* system quickly identifies the trouble spots, allowing management to establish a strategic inventory plan for flexible response to market demands.

ORIGIN OF THE *KANBAN* SYSTEM

The concept of the *kanban* system was developed by Taiichi Ohno of Toyota Motor Company after visiting a supermarket in the United States. As Ohno (1988) describes it, "We made a connection between supermarkets and the just-in-time system." He elaborates as follows:

> A supermarket is where a customer can get (1) what is needed, (2) at the time needed, (3) in the amount needed. Sometimes, of course, a customer may buy more than he or she needs. In principle, however, the supermarket is a place where we buy according to need. Supermarket operators, therefore, must make certain that customers can buy what they need *at any time.*
>
> From the supermarket, we got the idea of viewing the earlier process in a production line as a kind of store. The later process (customer) goes to the earlier process (supermarket) to acquire the required parts (commodities) at the time and in the quantity needed. The earlier process immediately produces the quantity just taken (restocking the shelves). We hoped that this would help us approach our just-in-time goal and, in 1953, we actually applied the system in our machine shop at the main plant.

THE 2-BIN *KANBAN* SYSTEM

One of the simplest kinds of *kanban* and perhaps the one most widely used is what's called a "2-bin *kanban* system." Figure 8.1

illustrates a simple 2-bin *kanban* system. An inventory specialist or other staff member creates this simple system by placing bins (in Figure 8.1, boxes) on a cart, although the bins could also be placed on shelves. Each bin contains one kind of part or item and is clearly labeled not only with information about the item inside (including the number of items in the bin), but also its location. This tells central supply where to deliver the box when it is refilled.

The key to the 2-bin system is that each box has a duplicate placed directly behind its twin. When the first bin is empty, that signals the person responsible for inventory to send the empty bin back to central supply to be refilled. The bin behind that one is then moved to the front of the cart and the item(s) inside is drawn from it. When the first box is refilled, it is placed behind the one currently being used.

Figure 8.1 A 2-Bin *Kanban* System

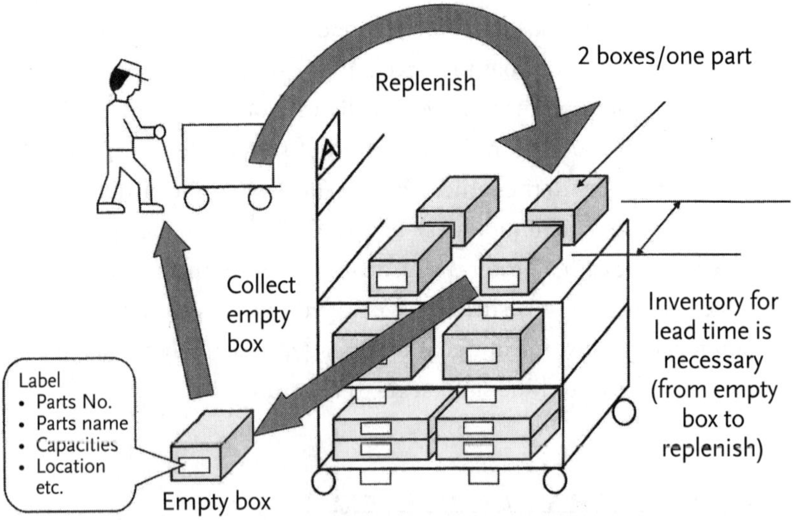

Source: Shingijutsu Global Consulting. Used with permission.

Knowing what constitutes a safe number of items on hand when the first box is empty is essential. This is known as the *par value* and depends largely on the demand for the item and the length of time needed to refill the bin.

If the quantity is set too high, an unnecessary level of inventory will result. If it's set too low, inventory shortages may occur. Koide and Iwata (2006) provide an example of how to determine an effective reorder point:

> Let's assume that the lead time is 10 days, daily usage is 2 pieces and ordered lot size is 20 pieces. In this case, inventory for production of 10 days must be maintained because of the 10-day lead time. The required quantity for inventory is 20 due to daily usage of 2 for 10 days. Therefore, it would seem that the proper timing to signal for the reorder is when inventory marks 20, because 20 pieces are delivered when 20 pieces are used.
>
> However, in the real world, it is the true state that such calculation would probably not serve because daily product volume will be changed slightly—even in the *heijunka* environment—and actual delivery time is variable, too. As a result, "buffer stock" must be allowed to absorb such variations. Buffer stock is usually set at 10–15 percent of delivered lot size, but it should be determined based on the actual variation. In this case, buffer stock is set at 2 pieces, using a 10 percent index and lot size of 20. Therefore, the reorder point becomes 22 (usage of 20 parts, plus the buffer stock of two.

Par level: In *kanban*, the level of supplies and inventory considered prudent to maintain on hand

Of course, you must periodically adjust these reorder points. Says Joe Hetzel, director of material services at Park Nicollet: "The 'par level'—the level of supplies and inventory we consider prudent to maintain on hand—changes as our services and processes change."

KANBAN AT PARK NICOLLET HEALTH SERVICES

According to Hetzel:

At Park Nicollet, we're using several different varieties of *kanban*. The most prevalent is the 2-bin system which we use for all our standard supplies, such as bandages, dressings, gauze, needles, and personal-care items. In the hospital, there are inventory specialists assigned to each floor. They check the bins from 2–3 times a week up to daily for heavy users of supplies.

The operating room has a *kanban* card attached to each product; the card is placed into an "on-order" post when the product

---

Figure 8.2 The *Kanban* Process Used at Park Nicollet's St. Louis Park Primary Care Clinic to Replenish Vials of a Hepatitis Medication

8.2(a) Using Medication *Kanban*

1 Identify medication bin

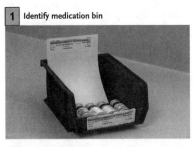

2 Acquire appropriate dose of med

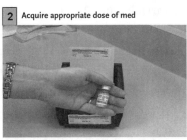

3 Once all meds in front of card are used, pull *kanban*

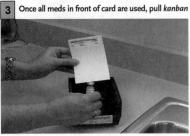

4 Place *kanban* in "*kanban* to be ordered" envelope

---

is used. An inventory specialist picks the card up from the holder on the post and gets the order filled within one day. In the catheter lab, an electronic version of *kanban* is used. When a product is used, the package barcode is scanned and downloaded to a hand-held scanning device. The information is then uploaded to a com-puterized inventory-management program, triggering reorder and replenishment of each supply item.

At Park Nicollet's primary care clinic at St. Louis Park, Minnesota, *kanban* is used to replenish medications. Figures 8.2a, 8.2b, and 8.2c show—via photographs and their descriptions—the 13 steps involved in setting up and maintaining a medication bin for vials of the drug Energix, used in the treatment of Hepatitis B.

8.2(b) Ordering from Medication *Kanban*

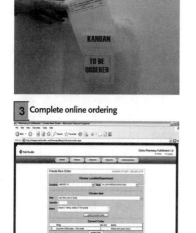

1 Pick up *kanban* from "*kanban* to be ordered" envelope

3 Complete online ordering

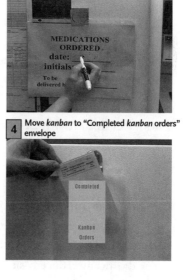

2 Document order

4 Move *kanban* to "Completed *kanban* orders" envelope

(Continued on following page)

8.2(c) Restocking Medication *Kanban*

1 Meds delivered via courier except Class II meds which are picked up by licensed staff

2 Enter lot numbers, check expiration dates

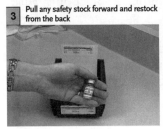

3 Pull any safety stock forward and restock from the back

4 Pull *kanban* from "Completed *kanban* orders" envelope

5 Replace *kanban* to appropriate bin(s)

Source: Park Nicollet Health Services. Used with permission.

Figure 8.3 shows in detail the label attached to the vials of Energix. When copies of the label are attached to simple 3-by-5 cards, they become the *kanban* cards used for reordering.

BENEFITS OF *KANBAN* IN THE HEALTHCARE SETTING

Park Nicollet Health Services

Again, according to Hetzel:

> Outages in *kanban* areas are virtually nil and defects in the form of purchasing errors—for example, wrong product ordered—have nearly been eliminated. Additionally, *kanban* has either eliminated or drastically reduced "sleeping inventory," or inventory that has largely been forgotten. In aggregate, the number of "par" items

Figure 8.3 Detail of the *Kanban* Card Used at Park Nicollet's St. Louis Park Primary Care Clinic to Replenish Vials of a Hepatitis Medication

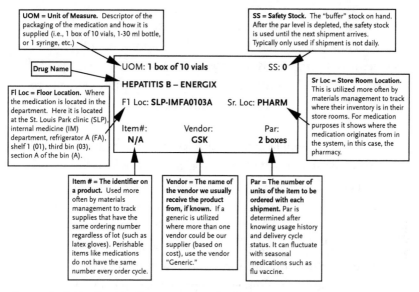

UOM = Unit of Measure. Descriptor of the packaging of the medication and how it is supplied (i.e., 1 box of 10 vials, 1-30 ml bottle, or 1 syringe, etc.)

SS = Safety Stock. The "buffer" stock on hand. After the par level is depleted, the safety stock is used until the next shipment arrives. Typically only used if shipment is not daily.

Drug Name

Fl Loc = Floor Location. Where the medication is located in the department. Here it is located at the St. Louis Park clinic (SLP), internal medicine (IM) department, refrigerator A (FA), shelf 1 (01), third bin (03), section A of the bin (A).

Sr Loc = Store Room Location. This is utilized more often by materials management to track where their inventory is in their store rooms. For medication purposes it shows where the medication originates from in the system, in this case, the pharmacy.

UOM: **1 box of 10 vials**   SS: **0**

HEPATITIS B – ENERGIX

Fl Loc: **SLP-IMFA0103A**   Sr. Loc: **PHARM**

Item#: **N/A**   Vendor: **GSK**   Par: **2 boxes**

Item # = The identifier on a product. Used more often by materials management to track supplies that have the same ordering number regardless of lot (such as latex gloves). Perishable items like medications do not have the same number every order cycle.

Vendor = The name of the vendor we usually receive the product from, if known. If a generic is utilized where more than one vendor could be our supplier (based on cost), use the vendor "Generic."

Par = The number of units of the item to be ordered with each shipment. Par is determined after knowing usage history and delivery cycle status. It can fluctuate with seasonal medications such as flu vaccine.

Source: Park Nicollet Health Services. Used with permission.

reduced inventory amounts by more than 50 percent. Furthermore, the *kanban* process has enabled us to manage inventory to the "point of use," resulting in a more accurate measure and control of inventory for each department.

Ancillary benefits include reducing walking distance for staff to obtain supplies by more than 70 percent and reducing inventory storage space by more than 50 percent. The creation and utilization of the "inventory specialist," in combination with value analysis, has led to greater product standardization and has identified opportunities to eliminate off-contract purchasing. These steps have led to an increased level of standardized products and greater contract compliance, further reducing our supply costs.

> **Sleeping inventory:** Inventory that has largely been forgotten

Finally, the *kanban* process has enabled us to reduce the number of inventory "touch points" from order entry to replenishment by more than 40 percent. Some people who used to be involved in the process are no longer involved at all.

Obviously, financial benefits flow from this increased efficiency as well: Park Nicollet has already realized approximately $250,000 in inventory savings across the hospital, catheterization lab, and clinics. But, as Hetzel points out, there are many more benefits to an effective *kanban* system than inventory cost savings alone:

> Movement of supplies and medicines are a key factor in overall patient and staff flow within the organization. When clinical staff are spending time hunting for supplies or medicines—or worse, when they're out of them—that slows the whole flow or stops it entirely. Obviously, this time is non–value-added for all concerned. Additionally, space in clinical areas is almost always limited. Therefore, efficient use of *kanban* will assist in increasing capacity, removing the defect of supply outages, and permit our professionals to focus on their clinical expertise.

Virginia Mason Medical Center

Virginia Mason Medical Center also can point to substantial benefits from the use of *kanban*, as Todd Johnson, vice president, describes:

> On the nursing units where we've implemented 2-bin supply-replenishment systems, we've seen up to a 30 percent reduction of inventories. In our central supply area, a similar 30 percent reduction from 2006 to 2007 has cut about $500,000 worth of inventory. Additionally, we've accomplished flat supply cost for the last two years, a time when significant cost escalation has been the norm.
>
> Our *kanban* systems have helped us avoid stock-outs, detect non–level-loaded supply demand, and adjust stock on hand.

THE IMPORTANCE OF *HEIJUNKA* AND *TAKT* TIME

As Hetzel points out: "*Kanban* works best in a defect-free environment where leveled production, or *heijunka*, has been achieved."

Recall from Chapter 4 that *heijunka* leads to the absence of bottlenecks—that is, processes working in concert. Think of it as even flow. If all the processes within a system are not working in pace with *takt* time, then the *kanban* system cannot work. Patients will wind up in queues or waiting for treatment with no provider present, or inventory will back up or run out at one or another point along the supply chain.

> **Even flow:** Processes working in concert with each other to prevent bottlenecks

LOCATION OF STORAGE AND KITTING

In some cases, replenishment from central supply may suffice. However, locating storage closer to the point of use, perhaps due to the critical nature of the item being stored, may be necessary. For example, clamps for arteries or veins should be stored where the end-user can see that there are sufficient supplies in storage.

The storage area may be a closet or a cart. In either case, storage boxes or bins should be labeled correctly with the item name and number, as well as identified by which shelf, rack, row, or column to store them on or in. The *kanban* cards must also contain this information so that the item to be replenished can be quickly and easily found.

If supplies are to be kitted (i.e., all materials needed at point of use put in a single container), the items in the kit box must be checked for accuracy and completeness. The kit boxes also must be identified clearly as described in the previous paragraph.

> **Kit:** All material needed at point of use put in a single container

POTENTIAL OBSTACLES

As with other Lean processes and tools, implementing a *kanban* system takes time and resources, and it requires adjustments from personnel. So, as with other Lean processes and tools, resistance may be encountered. A problem Hetzel encounters has to do with obtaining the staff he needs to implement *kanban* more extensively within Park Nicollet.

> While the benefits across the organization are clear, the benefit to any one department can be small and incremental. As a result, it is often difficult to get operations to transfer an FTE from any one department into material management to support *kanban* for the organization as a whole.

Overcoming resistance to pulling personnel from smaller units to support the greater good of the overall organization is a common problem within large organizations—and its solution requires leadership from the top. Top leaders must make clear to everyone in the organization that they are expected to operate with the health of the *overall organization* in mind, and that rewards and penalties will be allocated accordingly.

At Virginia Mason, Johnson says his biggest issue is "comprehensive staff training and education to ensure compliance with the system." One way he's working on gaining cooperation from staff is by "simplifying *kanban* so that the customers (nurses, medical assistants, etc.) have no responsibility for the success of the [*kanban*] system." Its success, instead, rests upon Johnson's system of inventory specialists.

EXTENDING *KANBAN* TO OUTSIDE SUPPLIERS

So far, this chapter has discussed how to replenish supplies from within a healthcare system. But obviously, your healthcare system will not be making its own scalpels, stents, or surgical gowns. This brings up the question of whether outside suppliers can and should be brought into *kanban* systems. The answer is *yes*. What's the point of maintaining an excellent *internal* resupply system if you can't count on receiving supplies when you need them from your *external* suppliers?

Figure 8.4 shows how such a system would work. The system is built upon a number of individual *kanban* processes, from supply of the patient room from the storage room, to the supply of the storage room from central supply, to the supply of central supply from various vendors.

Of course, as indicated in Figure 8.4, extending a *kanban* system to external suppliers requires not only the firm establishment of *kanban* systems within a healthcare system, but that suppliers have them as well. Extending *kanban* to a supplier is a time-consuming process, so it may come as no surprise that neither Virginia Mason nor Park Nicollet has accomplished this yet, although both are working with suppliers to extend *kanban* to their supply chains.

For example, Park Nicollet has included language defining Lean and *kanban* expectations in its contracts with its two largest suppliers. "First, however," Hetzel says, "these suppliers have to improve their own operations in a way that would support our *kanban* process. Both suppliers have initiated Lean programs and improvement work is underway. Plus, Park Nicollet has further improvements to make within our own operations before we can effectively collaborate with suppliers on Lean initiatives."

Says Johnson: "We're in discussion with our 'alpha vendor'—our largest supplier—regarding replenishment of the 2-bin *kanban*. There's also potential with our primary pharmaceutical vendor."

To get an idea of how powerful *kanban* and JIT can be for an organization when extended to suppliers, here's what one observer had to say about the network Toyota has created:

> Toyota stitched these networks—which were often made up of dozens of little suppliers—together using the same basic just-in-time principles it applied within the main factory. Later, Toyota's master manufacturing engineer, Taiichi Ohno, likened the resulting network to a "human body" in which "autonomic nerves" are able to react automatically to any distress. (Lynn 2005)

Figure 8.4 Operation of an Extended *Kanban* System

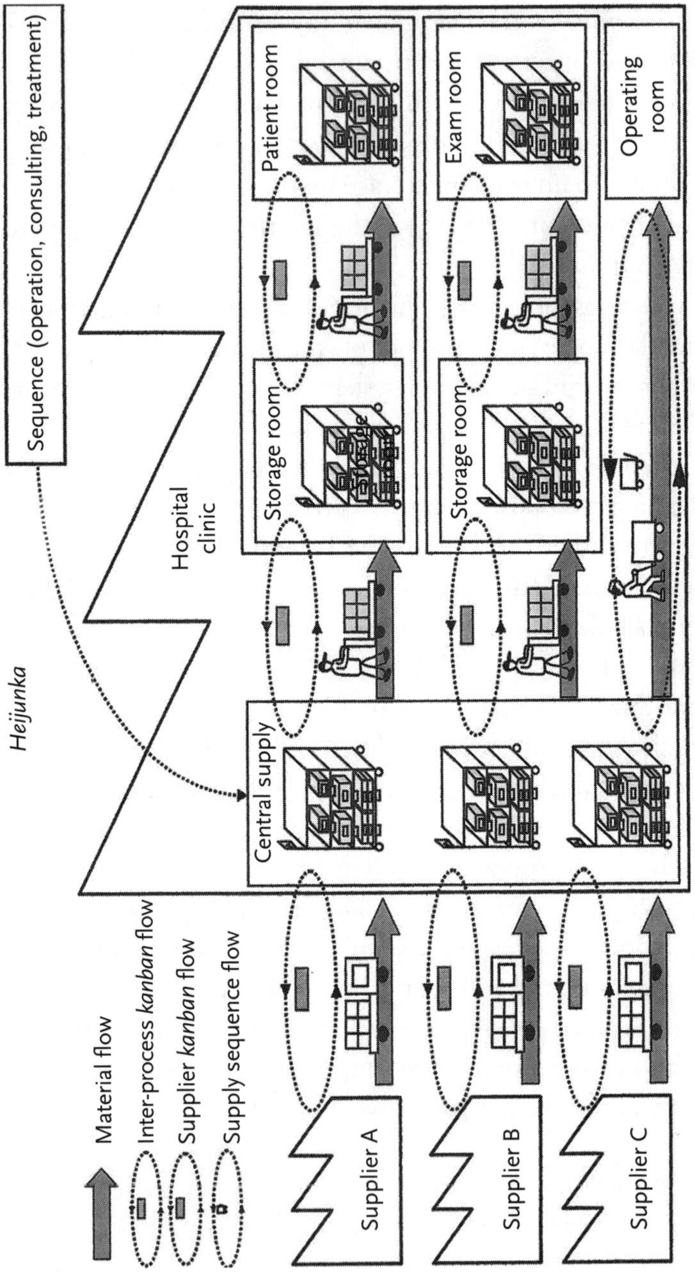

Heijunka

Sequence (operation, consulting, treatment)

Hospital clinic

Patient room

Exam room

Operating room

Storage room

Storage room

Central supply

Supplier A

Supplier B

Supplier C

Material flow
Inter-process *kanban* flow
Supplier *kanban* flow
Supply sequence flow

Source: Shingijjutsu Global Consulting. Used with permission.

CAPTURING THE FULL POTENTIAL OF YOUR *KANBAN* SYSTEM

A *kanban* system, like any other system, must be properly designed and maintained to capture the benefits sought. As Koide and Iwata (2006) warn:

> Since a *kanban* is merely one of the tools for just-in-time production, simply grafting a *kanban* system onto an existing production process does not automatically reduce costs. Only proper analysis, implementation, and maintenance of the *kanban* system can ensure that the full range of benefits available are realized.

Regarding maintenance, they say:

> The *kanban* is just a tool. Like any tool, a *kanban* system requires routine maintenance, such as reviewing the number of *kanbans* circulated and reorder points, etc., especially whenever production volume changes.

However, they go on to say:

> We also believe the *kanban* system's most valuable benefit is that operators and staff are given a tool with which to quickly identify and resolve abnormalities in a product or production process before it is passed to the next process. Indeed, the *kanban* system, when properly operated, will illuminate even hidden problems that affect overall efficiency and productivity. It is through these continuous improvement activities (*kaizen*) that staff and management become involved as problem-solvers, and thereby become the source of optimum quality assurance.

FINAL THOUGHTS

While implementing a system-wide *kanban* is challenging, doing so can make everyone's life easier, especially for those involved with the supply chain.

Says Hetzel:

> The important thing is that we're not running out of supplies anymore. I've been working in supply management for quite a few years. Lean has been professionally uplifting for me. *Kanban* has proven to be a highly effective Lean supply-chain tool. I'm convinced it's the right way to manage inventory.

And while *kanban* is a powerful weapon in fighting waste, its greatest payoff may be the assurance that when the surgeon asks the nurse for a vital instrument at a critical point in an operation, it will be there.

CHAPTER TAKEAWAYS

- *Kanban* is a pull JIT system of signaling when and where a patient service or supply item is needed, as well as when and where to restock inventory.
- The *kanban* system was developed by Taiichi Ohno of Toyota Motor Company after viewing the JIT system of a U.S. supermarket.
- A *kanban* system provides a superior tool for production control, visual management, and *kaizen*.
- The simplest and perhaps most widely used *kanban* system is the 2-bin system.
- *Kanban* has been used beneficially in various ways at Virginia Mason and Park Nicollet.
- Full implementation of a *kanban* system means extending it to outside suppliers.

REFERENCES

Koide, K., and T. Iwata. 2006. "Deployment of a Global *Kanban* System." Paper presented to the Aerospace Manufacturing and Automated Fastening Conference & Exhibition, Toulouse, France, September 12–14.

Lynn, B.C. 2005. *End of the Line: The Rise and Coming Fall of the Global Corporation*. New York: Doubleday.

Ohno, T. 1988. *Toyota Production System: Beyond Large-Scale Production*. New York: Productivity Press.

PART III

CASE EXAMPLES

CHAPTER 9

Lean Comes to
Virginia Mason Medical Center

OVERVIEW: This chapter examines in some detail how Lean came to Virginia Mason and how it is being implemented. It's important for the reader to gain a real-life sense of what's involved in implementing Lean. How do you get an organization to adopt Lean as its improvement strategy? How do you bring people on board? How do you put the Lean infrastructure in place? How do you even start? And perhaps most importantly, what results can you expect? Hopefully, this chapter will provide many of the answers.

IMPLEMENTING LEAN

A Chance Encounter

It was October 17, 2000, and I was on my way from Seattle, Washington, to Madrid, Spain, to meet with the Minister of Health to discuss how Spain could improve its healthcare system through the application of Lean. My presentation to him was in my laptop computer.

As I settled into my seat, the businessman beside me introduced himself as Mike Rona, president of Virginia Mason

Medical Center (VMMC). What an opportunity! Someone intimate with the healthcare field was right next to me, someone on whom I could try out my presentation. As we leveled out at 37,000 feet, I pulled out my laptop and said, "You really need to see this."

For the next hour, as I went through my PowerPoint® presentation, I believed I had his attention. When we headed for different connecting flights in Atlanta, I gave Rona a copy of my book *A World Class Production System.* Nonetheless, I figured I'd probably never hear from him again. He'd seemed interested, but everyone seems interested until they find out how much rigor and discipline Lean requires.

To my surprise, while still in Europe, I received an e-mail from Rona with more questions about Lean and then a phone call asking me to meet with Rona and his boss, Dr. Gary Kaplan, Virginia Mason's CEO. Unbeknownst to me, Rona had given Kaplan my book and, to my later surprise, I discovered he'd read through it a number of times.

When we met in early January 2001, I realized the depth of their interest and their willingness to take a tough approach to changing the way VMMC did business. Both Rona and Kaplan were all ears, enthusiastic about Lean and obviously committed to changing how Virginia Mason operated. It turned out that they were under pressure from the surgeons to build eight more operating rooms (ORs) at a cost of millions.

One of their challenges at the time was to increase OR capacity, but they didn't have the money to fund what was thought to be needed. They kept asking me, "How can we do it?" I told them capacity could be increased without a big expenditure, but only if they agreed to my plan.

The plan I had in mind for Virginia Mason was similar to the one we'd applied at Boeing. First, start by focusing at the point most vital to serving the customer (the patient). In the case of VMMC, that meant the OR. Second, define the value stream and designate a portion of that value stream as a model line, that is, an area of surgery where you could drill down a mile deep and an inch wide. Third, create a KPO and establish the infrastructure to support *kaizen*.

New Paradigms Needed

Later I sent both Kaplan and Rona an e-mail identifying two paradigm shifts necessary to achieve the results in the surgery department (and elsewhere) that they wanted:

1. *Consider the OR a profit center rather than a cost center.*
   Traditional measures of OR performance focus on costs, ignoring the fact that surgery success is foremost a matter of creating defect-free outcomes that eliminate waste. The result is higher quality and maximized revenues. In other words, *focus on the patient by improving quality and you'll make money.*
2. *Imagine capacity expansion without spending money, adding people, or creating additional space.* Take bolder but less dramatic actions to identify and eliminate waste, thereby increasing throughput.

Kaplan and Rona had no problem making the mental leap from manufacturing to healthcare. They simply said, "We're going to do it."

On February 27, 2001, Kaplan and Rona issued the first of many communications on moving forward. They sent a letter to the top 36 Virginia Mason leaders stating,

At the medical center level, we have identified three areas upon which we wish to begin our focus: perioperative services, gastroenterology, and the emergency department. The reasons we are focusing on these areas is that they are extremely busy, in great demand, need solutions urgently to accommodate demand, and are key departments related to margin achievement.

They also emphasized that all leaders were expected to attend a two-day executive workshop on March 26 and 27.

Setting the Bar

A workshop was conducted, which, at that time, was led by me and my associates—Japanese-trained former executives from Boeing. Kaplan's comments at the end of the session challenged the leaders and left some extremely worried about the direction Kaplan and Rona were taking Virginia Mason, particularly the aggressive targets they were setting. (I considered them right on the money.)

> It has never been more apparent that now the time is ripe for change at VMMC. These last two days we have experienced an incredible amount of tension—good tension—about our organization. Nothing is off limits. The message to take away today is that we are not advocating working faster. We are, however, advocating not increasing space or people and spending more money. We are also advocating a new way to set targets and to achieve the results—the discipline of Lean and the Toyota Production System using Rapid Process Improvement Workshops. John Black and Associates will be our consultants. Mike and I are committed to the long term to change the way we manage Virginia Mason. The targets for this year are to decrease lead time 50 percent in surgery scheduling, reduce costs per case 30 percent, and increase throughput to 25,000 cases per year in 24 months.

For some, the air had just been sucked out of the room. There was much discussion and debate with Kaplan, and a testing of his resolve to stick with the targets as the two-day session ended. It was obvious that initially many were not on board with the direction Kaplan and Rona wanted to take VMMC.

Getting Started

The first year is always difficult. This would be no exception. The first Rapid Process Improvement Workshop the week of April 23 to 27 consisted of four teams with aggressive targets:

- Team 1: Standardize laparoscopic case carts with one standard cart for all surgeons and achieve a 50 percent reduction in returned items.
- Team 2: Create a laparoscopic cell (work area) for check-in through surgery with a 50 percent reduction in patient waiting time and a 50 percent reduction in space.
- Team 3: Create a one-piece flow cell for pre-operative charts with a 90 percent defect reduction.
- Team 4: Standardize the room-preparation process for all surgeries with the target of standard work in place and the patient out to room ready in five minutes.

The results were excellent for the kickoff effort, but the real learning of the week, as reported by VMMC, was "that teams of process-knowledgeable people could make a major change in a one-week period." For example, Team 1 reduced surgical instruments on the case cart from 74 to 58 items for an annual savings of $26,880. The organization of the OR equipment room was totally redesigned for easier access, visual control, and location of equipment. Team 2 created a laparoscopic cell that reduced space 25 percent, walking distance 75 percent, patient lead time 54 percent, and wait time 69 percent. Teams 3 and 4 experienced similar results. This initial success set the stage for aggressive continued workshop events.

My message to those involved in these first Lean efforts was that we would be taking "two steps forward and one step backward and to keep trusting the process," because it is powerful and works. "The key here is building momentum, passion, and carrying through so this process begins to have a life of its own. Remember, we are dealing with the inertia of organization, the behavior that goes with it, and the resistance to change that is typical in all organizations."

The next move was to start hammering on the importance of infrastructure. My emphasis was the same as it had been at Boeing and would be for Park Nicollet later on. I told the Virginia Mason leaders that:

- VMMC needed a strong Lean leader certification program for the top 36 managers and their direct reports;
- VMMC needed a visibility room to make the right metrics accessible to those who needed to measure Lean progress;
- the rigor of the RPIW process needed to be followed and maintained by the workshop leaders in certification;
- middle management needed to take on the job of breaking down barriers and following up on implementation; and
- middle managers also had to stay focused on the business strategy of big targets aimed at major reductions in lead time and increased throughput—and they had to follow up, follow up, and follow up.

Reaffirming the Commitment

Kaplan and Rona had issued what they called "The Mandate for Rapid Change" on April 30, 2001. This document challenged Virginia Mason leaders to "Initiate a major organization-wide frontal assault on waste and the unnecessary, non–value-added variation that is rampant in our organization." A major business reality facing VMMC and communicated in their mandate addressed the intense payer pressure driving healthcare-cost reductions. As the mandate stated, "The business environment is extremely hostile. Reimbursement does not cover our growing expenses. Increased reliance on costly technology and new medications drives up costs."

Kaplan and Rona made the need for change clearer still:

This is not a crisis, but will be one unless we change very soon. We need to commit ourselves, organizationally, to operate as a successful business. This is what we need from everyone in the organization: understanding of our situation and the need to make rapid improvements; commitment to help achieve our financial goals by identifying opportunity, reducing waste and working smarter; honesty about what you're facing and what you need to be successful; innovation and fresh thinking about long standing problems; flexibility and willingness to change.

Resistance and the First Japan Trip

As we prepared for our first trip to Japan, it was apparent to me that not everyone was on board. Kaplan and Rona were getting calls from some Virginia Mason leaders questioning their judgment. Prior to the trip, an article appeared on the front page of *The Seattle Times*, talking about the folly and cost of VMMC going to Japan. As usual, Virginia Mason communications staff handled the matter well. They invited the reporter to come to VMMC and understand why its leaders considered the Japan trip worth the cost.

Prep sessions for the trip began on April 25 with a visit to Genie-Terex Industries in Redmond, Washington, where hydraulic lifts, such as forklifts, are made. The Virginia Mason team was required to move through the factory sketching the seven *factory* flows (flow of people, information, equipment, engineering, raw materials, work in process, and finished product).

The Japan trip from June 19 to July 3, 2002, was a great success. Those on the trip included Kaplan and Rona, their direct reports, board members, leaders involved in the *kaizen* certification process, and others. All senior executives had been required to go on this Japan trip, including physician executives. On the last day, at the Imperial Hotel in Tokyo, Kaplan and Rona threw down the gauntlet by announcing that, henceforth, VMMC would be implementing the Virginia Mason Production System (VMPS).

The response was energy, excitement, shock, and some skepticism. It was clear there was no immediate consensus in the room to move forward as aggressively as Kaplan and Rona planned.

Virginia Mason's *Kaizen* Action Plan

A plan was published immediately and sent to all concerned at VMMC, with instructions from Kaplan and Rona to start the planning process. Highlights included the following:

- Reemphasize that the patient comes first, using "Patient First" as the driver for all that we do. We have a great strategic plan with Lean thinking as a foundational element. This plan is only strengthened by what we have learned during our visit to Japan. By declaring "Patient First," we will make our commitment visible in our training and in our physical environment.
- Declare our brand of Lean to be VMPS, which will have several implications: This will be our management method and RPIWs will be our major *kaizen* methodology. Value-stream maps will be developed for inpatients, outpatients, procedure areas, and all major divisions of the organization by October 1, 2002. This will assist us in targeting areas for improvement in the budgeting process for 2003.
- Create an environment in which our people feel safe and free to engage in improvement.
- We will ensure education and training on the Virginia Mason Production System throughout the organization. All executive leaders will be certified as trainers by January 1, 2003. All trainers will devote 50 percent of their time to Lean efforts. All executive leaders must have participated in at least one RPIW by the end of 2002. Fifty percent of all staff will have been trained in the one-day "Introduction to Lean" class by December 31, 2002.
- Implement a companywide, defect-alert system (a *jidoka* system). We will have in place a system whereby all of our staff feel that it is their obligation, on behalf of our patients, to let us know when any kind of defect is occurring. Change our risk management department to a patient safety department by September 1, 2002.

- Create a prosperous economic organization. We have learned that there is waste in all of our processes and we know that as we reduce waste, we see improvements in quality, customer satisfaction, staff satisfaction, safety, and economics. It is our intent to steadily reduce the cost per unit of production in the years to come:
  - reduce cost per unit of service by 10 percent in 2003;
  - apply Lean practices before adding any people, space, or equipment;
  - aggressively work with suppliers to provide us with the exact products we need, when and where we need them, and in the right amounts; continue to build our rigorous supply chain management system; and
  - reduce inventory by 50 percent by the end of 2003.
- Require leadership accountability. The entire leadership team of VMMC is committed to, and responsible for, the implementation of all of the above, with the executive leadership group leading the effort.
- Compensation for all leadership for 2002 will be aligned with the above expectations, competency in the VMPS, and the overall performance of our organization.

Confronting Waste

The first RPIW that Rona participated in focused on the emergency department. He was shocked. He said to me, "I didn't realize how bad things were." I replied that his shock is typical of high-level leaders in organizations.

You've spent most of your time leading from the comfort of your office and now you are seeing the *muda*—the waste and confusion—your hard-working people deal with everyday. Your patients are subjects of a disservice when the leaders are not involved at the grassroots level of ferreting out the waste and leading from the hospital floor instead of from the comfort of the executive suite.

More and more leaders completed the Lean leader certification program. Participants were serious, enthusiastic, and highly motivated. Rona's can-do attitude and challenging personal style were keeping pressure on the organization as it moved toward some semblance of VMPS. Candidates for certification, from CEO Kaplan on down the chain of command, were required to complete the process with a score of at least three ("stand-alone capable of planning and leading a workshop, to include presenting all workshop training modules").

I continued to stress the importance of *sketching* for those in certification. Candidates were all required to go out into the medical center and sketch the seven flows of medicine (as covered in detail in Chapter 7). They were then required to present examples of their sketches. I then told them how a study of Leonardo da Vinci's sketches had helped Toyota's consultants and engineers better understand the concept of flow.

Sketching: A technique of Lean where participants observe and sketch Lean in action

Raising the Bar

In November 2002, I sent Kaplan a list of what Virginia Mason should have in place by December 2003, as we continued to roll out the many elements of Lean.

1. Standard work a practice in key business areas.
2. All RPIWs focused on the right targets.
3. Report-outs clear and disciplined, forms used, results immediate.
4. Visibility room operating and used to drive Lean.
5. Administrative directors and leadership team leading three workshops a year.

6. VMMC moving from a functionally driven to a product-driven, service-line organization.
7. Hiring stopped, redeployment routine.
8. The equation of *Profit = Price – Cost* in place, in practice.
9. Every team member a "waste-ologist."
10. Management layers reduced.
11. Anchor draggers removed from the organization.

Taking Stock

On January 7, 2003, Kaplan and Rona convened a half-day meeting at the Sorrento Hotel in Seattle with all members of the executive leadership team who had gone to Japan the previous year. Comments from everyone indicated that a paradigm shift in thinking had taken place and that a transformation to VMPS *would happen*. The transformational power of the certification process the leaders had been through, culminating in the Japan trip, was evident. Below is a sampling of comments:

- Anesthesiologists now engaged in planning and incorporating projects, amazing; I am feeling uplifted.
- Good job in introducing Lean. Physicians say we have legitimized RPIWs.
- We have started to change the culture and language.
- Patient-first safety is taking hold. Certification of executives gets five stars.
- People following Lean principles have seen it in the budget.
- Going to Japan made the difference in thinking.
- Need to spend more time looking at value-stream maps.
- We need to do a better job of leading by example.
- Biggest challenge is pushing this down, another order of magnitude in middle management.
- We have a gap between this team and section heads and doctors.

- When we operate like a symphony it is extraordinary.
- Doing well but at times we are drowning.

Auditing and Accelerating Progress

In January 2004, Virginia Mason's *Kaizen* Promotion Office (KPO) completed an assessment, or internal audit, to determine the status of progress and challenges in all major areas of VMPS implementation. The audit covered certification, Lean mastery, the conduct of RPIWs, report-outs, the Japan trip, model lines, the standard work alert system, the KPO structure, the deployment of standard operations (working to customer requirements of *takt* time, standard work, and standard work-in-process), and other Lean elements.

> **Standard operations:**
> Working to customer requirements of *takt* time, standard work, and standard work-in-process

I reviewed a copy of the audit and sent my own analysis to Rona. The KPO assessment confirmed my own view of Virginia Mason's Lean progress over the past two years. While much improvement had occurred, the pace was too slow. To help propel the organization forward, the basic policy of the Toyota Production System that VMMC leaders had learned in Japan was reviewed, and I added my own twist to Toyota's policy.

1. Take action based on *kaizen* needs, not action based on political expediency.
2. Challenge what you should do with the patient in mind, rather than what you can do.
3. Do *kaizen*, not other things that may be easier.
4. Chase the root cause with a passion and vengeance.
5. If you have an idea, take immediate action; you may forget it by tomorrow.

6. Do motion *kaizen* before equipment *kaizen*; monuments can be moved later.
7. After the course of action is decided, make sure safety and quality are covered.

Kicking into Higher Gear: The Right *Kaizen* Promotion Office

Finally, in December 2004, what I had been advocating for months and months in terms of the right KPO and the right leaders to make it effective was established by Rona and Kaplan. The purpose of the new structure was to accelerate the impact and application of the Virginia Mason Production System (VMPS) to the operations of VMMC.

The VMPS *Kaizen* Production Office would consist of three decentralized KPO implementation units—clinic, corporate, and hospital—with each KPO unit responsible for creating the value-stream map, setting targets, and achieving those targets. The senior vice presidents and appropriate chief medical partners would be responsible for the clinic and hospital KPOs, respectively.

The corporate KPO would report to Christina Saint Martin, vice president, KPO, and she would report to Rona. Each KPO's executive leaders and administrative directors would direct the goals of the unit, which had to be consistent with overall medical-center goals. The leaders of each KPO unit were responsible for directing, prioritizing, and ensuring implementation of all Lean activities within the scope of their unit. These leaders were also responsible for submission of KPO implementation plans to Virginia Mason's administration division for review and comment and/or approval (in the case of the corporate KPO implementation unit).

Since these changes were made, VMMC's progress toward Lean has accelerated greatly, as the results below demonstrate.

RESULTS AT VIRGINIA MASON PROVE LEAN WORKS

2002 to 2004

As Saint Martin says, "We'd studied validated industry results from use of the Toyota Production System, but we were not absolutely convinced we have 50 percent or more waste in our processes until we looked at the big picture and actually assembled the results."

The RPIWs held from 2002 to 2004 yielded the following gains in the areas selected for improvement:

- 24 percent reduction in the space needed
- 51 percent reduction in inventory
- 38 percent reduction in staff walking distance
- 77 percent reduction in parts travel distance
- 53 percent reduction in patient lead time
- 62 percent reduction in standard work-in-process
- 47 percent reduction in quality defects
- 44 percent gain in productivity
- 83 percent reduction in setup time

2005

In 2005, Virginia Mason began to view results at an organizational level that would reflect the overall company performance improvement in clinic volumes, length of stay in the hospital, cash on hand, and defects. For the first time, VMMC set very specific goals and targets for improvement work that the entire management team at VMMC would be held accountable to achieve. All of the KPO resources were aligned to achieve those results.

The target areas and results from 2005 yielded the following results in the selected areas for improvement:

- 85 percent reduction in lead time in the surgery supply distribution process
- 63 percent reduction in lead time in the surgery billing cycle
- 29 percent reduction in overtime and temporary labor in overhead areas
- 40 percent reduction in number of products on surgical procedure cards
- 63 percent reduction in patient lead time for the satellite clinic primary care visit
- 43 percent patient reduction in lead time in the screening colonoscopy process
- 100 percent reduction in medication and solution labeling errors in the clinic
- 94 percent improvement in patient summary list completion
- 6 percent reduction in hospital average length of stay
- 10 percent improvement in total hospital labor efficiency

2006

The target areas and results from 2006 yielded the following results in the selected areas for improvement:

- 4 percent reduction in patient lead time for the inpatient medical stay
- 9 percent reduction in lead time for a surgical inpatient stay
- 7 percent reduction in lead time in the emergency department
- 35 percent reduction in lead time in ambulatory care visits
- 98 percent reduction in lead time for gastroenterology procedural services
- 62 percent reduction in lead time for the revenue cycle
- 50 percent reduction in emergency department diverts
- 100 percent reduction in incomplete medication or solution identification

- 78 percent improvement in surgical pause standard work
- 9 percent improvement in bed turns
- 4 percent improvement in patient cash receipts

The obvious conclusion: Lean works! In the next chapter, you will read about two model lines at Virginia Mason—the cancer center and the hyperbaric clinic—to learn in more detail how Lean can improve a healthcare service line's operations.

CHAPTER TAKEAWAYS

- Virginia Mason Medical Center began its Lean journey in early 2001 when CEO Mike Kaplan and President Mike Rona announced that Lean would be VMMC's improvement system and set stretch improvement targets.
- Four *kaizen* events that spring proved the power of Lean.
- Consistent reinforcement of the message that top leaders were serious about implementing Lean, and their involvement in improvement activities, helped overcome staff resistance.
- The implementation of the *right* KPO and supporting units in 2004 helped speed progress.
- Results since 2002 have been dramatic.

CHAPTER 10

Virginia Mason Medical Center
Case Studies

OVERVIEW: The two case studies in this chapter demonstrate the value of building Lean from the ground up by applying it to selected service lines and making them your model lines. The model lines not only then constitute parts of your health-care organization where Lean has been extensively implemented, but, as the name implies, serve as models for other services lines (and functional departments). As you'll see, although both model lines in this chapter applied the tools and principles of Lean, they applied them differentially depending on their unique needs.

The benefit of any improvement process, including Lean, naturally rests in the results it produces. Throughout this book, I've provided numerous examples of improvements to individual processes or activities within Virginia Mason Medical Center and Park Nicollet Health Services. However, the transformative potential of Lean is only fully actualized when you link all of the small, incremental improvements (*kaizen*) with the larger, more radical improvements (*kaikaku*) into an overall, organization-wide production system.

Major building blocks along the way are the model lines, where an entire service line or functional department undergoes both *kaizen* and *kaikaku* toward overall improvement of that organization. They are also important evidence of the synergistic power of Lean when an array of Lean processes and tools is applied to an entire service line or functional department.

Two model lines at VMMC demonstrate this power. (Chapter 12 will introduce you to three more from Park Nicollet.)

CANCER INSTITUTE

VMMC's cancer institute consists of hematology oncology, radiation oncology, an infusion center, a cancer registry, an inpatient cancer care unit, and 11 cancer service lines (e.g., breast, prostate, pancreatic).

On January 8, 2004, eight members of the institute came together to kick off the "Cancer Model Line." They were excited and ready for major change. (Previously, all eight had traveled to Japan as part of their extensive certification process.) In the group were Dr. Andrew Jacobs, the institute's chief, and administrative directors Denise Dubuque, RN, and Julie Sylvester. These three, along with Dr. Henry Otero, section head for hematology oncology, would provide key leadership for the planned change to Lean operations.

Many of the institute's staff were excited about the planned move to new, larger, and better quarters on the eleventh floor of a building adjacent to the hospital, where the institute was then housed. On the other hand, the idea of changing the way work was performed was viewed with some reservation. However, the overall medical center leadership was committed to Lean, and the cancer institute and the hyperbaric clinic had been selected as the first two model lines.

Just as the medical center had a vision, so did the cancer institute: "To be the quality leader in cancer care." To actualize this vision, the team identified the following five goals:

1. Put the patient first.
2. Implement the Virginia Mason Production System.

3. Strive for zero defects.
4. Attain high staff satisfaction.
5. Achieve strong economic performance.

Another of the team's goals was to increase the number of cancer patients Virginia Mason could treat (17,000 per year, with approximately 2,000 new each year). The team quickly realized the solution to improved patient care wasn't just a new facility—not even the one they'd been anticipating, with lovely views of Seattle and Puget Sound. The solution was improving the processes and flow of the patients to provide the highest quality experience.

3P, Standard Work, and the New Facility

Every process must operate within the space available. But, according to Lean principles, the process also must achieve the primary end of providing fast, effective, and high-quality service to the customer—in this case, the cancer patient. It didn't take long for the model-line leadership team, working through 3P (production preparation process) with spaghetti charts (diagrams of patient and staff flow), to realize that the space with the fine views was working against their goal of minimizing patient and staff travel time.

Spaghetti chart: A diagram of patient and staff flow

This is where the team's top principle of "put the patient first" was tested. The more functional location, because of proximity to radiation oncology, radiology, and surgical services, turned out to be space on the second floor of the older clinic building. Not only did this alternative location lack grand views, but 3P identified that the best way to serve patients was to provide them the window rooms and locate staff in the middle of the available space. Not only no grand views, but no views at all for the physicians—except when seeing patients. Altruism reigned when the staff gave up the space most to their liking for one that served patients better.

Although staff accepted this unanticipated result of Lean graciously (if regretfully), they were more resistant to the concept of standard work. "We do not manufacture cars; we treat people," is the way Dr. Jacobs characterizes the way many clinicians initially reacted. "Medical people generally have a 'craftsman' mentality," he explains.

A series of *kaizen* events helped break down this resistance. Participants soon saw how standardization of support services (and not provider-patient interaction or treatment regimes) provided superior patient care. As Dr. Jacobs reminded all involved in Lean, "It's not standard work we're after, but gold standard work."

Another aid in overcoming resistance was the continual mantra by the leadership team that "Change is hard, but the status quo is unacceptable."

The new facility—the Floyd & Delores Jones Cancer Institute—opened in January 2005 (Figure 10.1).

Figure 10.1

The entrance to Virginia Mason's new Floyd & Delores Jones Cancer Institute.

Source: Virginia Mason Medical Center. Used with permission.

Applying Lean Principles and Tools

Besides 3P and standard work, the cancer institute applied many other Lean principles and tools, including defining the value stream and *takt* time, mistake-proofing, and, in particular, load leveling (*heijunka*). One of the ways both radiation oncology and the infusion center went about leveling the load was to apply the concept of cascade scheduling (i.e., staggering start times for patients and staff). This enabled both clinics to offer longer hours of operation to patients (resulting in increased patient volume) without burning out staff, as well as to maximize availability of needed equipment. For example, the infusion center gained nearly two hours per treatment station just from moving to a cascade schedule.

In addition to cascade scheduling, radiation oncology focused on reducing radiation treatment setup times for patients. One way was to provide an on-deck chair outside the treatment room to accommodate the next

> **Cascade Scheduling:**
> Staggering start times for patients and staff

patient waiting for treatment, which decreased room idle time and shortened the patient's lead time. Another was to provide the therapist a work zone within the treatment room. As a result of all the Lean improvements, radiation oncology accomplished the following:

- 14 percent reduction in the patient's lead time (arrival to completion of treatment),
- 57 percent increase in the number of patients treated per therapist, and
- 61 percent reduction in staff walking distance.

These improvements also resulted in reduced employee overtime, while creating the capacity for increased patient volume. In addition, to address safety issues, Virginia Mason as an organization instituted patient safety alerts (PSAs) as part of its system of *jidoka*. As mentioned

Table 10.1 Ted Gachowski's Pre-Lean Schedule

8:00–8:05 a.m.	Arrive at Virginia Mason, check in at lobby
8:05–8:30 a.m.	Arrive at laboratory after several elevator rides and long hallways (distance traveled: 119 feet)
8:30–10:15 a.m.	Check in for doctor's appointment, wait for lab results, complete doctor's appointment (distance traveled: 200 feet)
10:15–11:00 a.m.	Several more elevator rides and long hallways, check in for chemotherapy treatment (distance traveled: 441 feet)
11:00–11:15 a.m.	Wait for chemotherapy treatment room to be vacant, walk to treatment room, wait for an RN (distance traveled: 526 feet)
11:15 a.m.–12:00 p.m.	Start IV, pre-meds, symptom review; wait for chemotherapy to be delivered; start chemotherapy (distance traveled: 526 feet)
12:00–6:25 p.m.	Complete chemotherapy, several more elevator rides and more long hallways to exit VMMC (distance traveled: 748 feet)
SUMMARY	10:25 hours at the hospital, including lead time of 4 hours Distance traveled: 748 feet Non–value-added time: 3:14 hours

by Virginia Mason CEO Gary Kaplan in the foreword to this book, VMMC's PSA system encourages any employee to halt any process if he believes something has gone wrong. As Dr. Jacobs says, "Incorporating PSAs has enabled us to catch 'near-misses' and make process improvements."

Table 10.2 Ted Gachowski's Schedule After Lean

8:00–8:05 a.m.	Check in at lobby
8:05–8:10 a.m.	Elevator to second floor (distance traveled: 18 feet)
8:10–8:15 a.m.	Check in at clinic, walk to treatment room (distance traveled: 105 feet)
8:15–9:35 a.m.	In treatment room, RN admission, lab draw, doctor visit, access to scheduler while being treated (distance traveled: 105 feet)
9:35 a.m.–3:40 p.m.	Complete chemotherapy (distance traveled: 105 feet)
3:40–3:45 p.m.	Exit hospital (distance traveled: 181 feet)
SUMMARY	7:45 hours at the hospital, including lead time of 1:30 hours Distance traveled: 181 feet Non–value-added time: 52 minutes

A Day in the Life of Ted Gachowski

It's difficult to understand improvements in purely statistical terms. Let's take a look at the difference Lean operations can make to a patient. That patient is Ted Gachowski, a retired engineer who has suffered from lymphoma since 1999. Every week, he makes a three-hour drive from his home to receive a six-hour chemotherapy treatment in the cancer institute. Usually, because of the long day, he stays overnight in Seattle.

Before the move to the new facility and before Lean operations, Ted's visit to the institute followed the schedule outlined in Table 10.1. Table 10.2 shows the difference the new facility and Lean have made.

So, Lean has cut Ted's time at the hospital by 2 hours and 40 minutes (25 percent), his lead time by 2 hours and 30 minutes (63 percent), his travel distance by 567 feet (76 percent), and his non–value-added time in the hospital by 142 minutes (73 percent). And this is true of every other cancer patient at VMMC.

Some Overall Results

Ted Gachowski's story illustrates the value of putting the patient first. It's also good business, as some other results for the institute's improvement plan for 2006, as compared with 2005, show:

- The number of patients treated in the infusion center increased by 8 percent (with the same number of staff).
- The radiation oncology unit exceeded its revenue target by $1 million.
- Patient satisfaction is in the 95th percentile.
- Staff satisfaction is in the 93rd percentile.

Learnings

Change was difficult for staff, but not for patients.

As Dr. Otero says, "All staff resistance boils down to fear of change. Everyone fears that a change will make things worse or that their work is being examined." He also admits, "There's a period when things get worse before they get better. The first six months after the changeover, morale dipped, but after a while you smooth out the rough edges." Regarding this concern, administrative director Dubuque says: "A lot of communication is needed. The leadership team needs to be out on the floor. It also has to be prepared to make adjustments quickly." She adds, "The patients seemed to have no problem accepting the changes."

Small changes can lead to big improvements.

This is part of what *senseis* call "just doing it." The most important part is "trialing rather than continually planning," according to Dubuque, "and being willing to accept failure." Dr. Jacobs quotes Von Clausewitz, the famous military thinker: "The greatest enemy of a good idea is the dream of a perfect plan."

Don't let your improvement teams set easy targets.

According to Dr. Jacobs, a number of teams at Virginia Mason "needed greater stretch goals. There was too much focus on 'low-hanging fruit'" (i.e., the easiest improvement opportunities).

Never underestimate the value of simulation.

As Dr. Otero points out, it was simulation of the space that led the cancer institute to choose a more efficient and effective space for their services. "I would never underestimate the value of simulation. Do more of it, even in Rapid Process Improvement Workshops."

Deploy production boards and visual controls right away.

It's critical for people to see what progress they are making. This requires making progress visible where people work—part of daily management.

It's important to focus on Lean principles instead of tools and methods.

The first principle, of course, is putting the customer (i.e., patient) first. Other principles the cancer institute emphasized were removing waste (*muda*) and implementing continuous flow, pull production, and continuous incremental improvement (*kaizen*).

You have to be persistent.

The improvement leadership team kept this Japanese proverb in mind: "If you fall down seven times, get up eight." Another way to say it is, "Take two steps forward and one back."

Figure 10.2

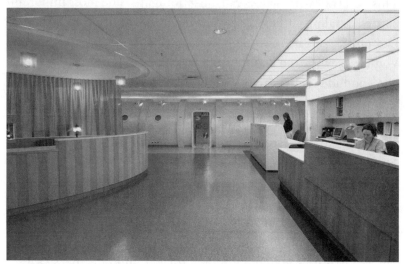

The entrance to Virginia Mason's new Center for Hyperbaric Medicine

Source: Virginia Mason Medical Center. Used with permission.

THE CENTER FOR HYPERBARIC MEDICINE

To enter Virginia Mason's Center for Hyperbaric Medicine (Figure 10.2) is to enter a healthcare environment almost certainly unlike any you've experienced before. Imagine a clinic as peaceful and quiet as a library, as clean and uncluttered as a computer-server room, and as spacious and attractive as the lobby of a five-star hotel—one with neither patients nor staff moving about aimlessly or frantically. That's VMMC's Center for Hyperbaric Medicine.

"Visitors are always asking where everyone is," says the center's medical director, Dr. Neil Hampson. "They're here being treated in one of our hyperbaric chambers or in an examination room or some other location out of the public eye."

Sound too luxurious to be affordable? What if you were told that this new clinic is extremely profitable? It is. And patients and staff love it.

> **What Does a Hyperbaric Clinic Do?**
>
> A hyperbaric clinic provides 100 percent oxygen, as opposed to the 21 percent oxygen in the air we normally breathe, to patients in an environment where the air pressure is two to six times that outside the chamber to infuse oxygen into patients' blood and tissue. The combination of oxygen-rich blood and tissue and heavy air pressure has proven effective in repairing injured tissue (including from radiation therapy), in treating air/gas embolism and "the bends" (nitrogen bubbles in tissue), and in treating gas gangrene and carbon monoxide poisoning, among other beneficial uses.

The Way It Was

Before telling you more about this amazing success story, let's go back to a time when the current facility didn't exist. Pre-history, Dr. Hampson may tell you, although you only have to go back to 2004 to enter a completely different era.

Virginia Mason's hyperbaric clinic began in 1969 as a research facility across the street from the main hospital, with a four-patient hyperbaric chamber and a one-patient monochamber added in 1970 (Figure 10.3).

Although the research facility became a clinical facility in 1980, the physical layout of the facility and the chambers remained the same. Certainly, there was nothing futuristic about the facility. The waiting room consisted of a couple of wooden chairs in the hallway, the dressing room was a public bathroom, and there was very little privacy in the patient-assessment area, where patients had their blood pressure taken and were prepared for the hyperbaric treatment.

To make matters worse, because of federal regulations, patients had to travel from the main hospital, where they checked in, to the hyperbaric clinic across the street by ambulance (costly as that was). There, they exited the ambulance and walked into the clinic exposed to the elements, often having to push their way through people waiting in the same location for the city bus.

Figure 10.3

Virginia Mason's previous one- and four-patient hyperbaric chambers.

Source: Virginia Mason Medical Center. Used with permission.

The four-patient chamber, with the required attendant inside, was hardly a comfortable treatment space. Patients had to climb a couple of stairs to get inside, squeeze through a tiny doorway, and seat themselves on metal folding chairs. There they would sit, cramped together in an eight-foot-diameter chamber, until their two-hour (on average) treatment was over. Both patients and staff often suffered from ergonomic complaints from the uncomfortable chairs and lack of space.

At the same time, since the clinic had been forced into the only space available in the research facility, the layout followed no particular method or plan. Patients and staff walked back and forth between locations in a pattern more like a bowl of spaghetti than a straight line. Similarly, records, supplies, and the other necessities of the clinic were sited in almost random fashion.

Furthermore, the ongoing demand for the clinic's services outgrew its capacity to meet the demand. To treat all the patients, the clinic had to stay open 12 to 14 hours a day, requiring a second shift on per diem. Wait times for routine treatment could extend as long as eight weeks. Even then, emergencies frequently bumped patients from their scheduled routine treatments. As a result, patients and prospective patients often wound up going somewhere else for treatment.

A New Clinic and a New Way of Doing Things

Early in this decade Virginia Mason decided to construct a new hyperbaric facility at a cost of $7.1 million.

Fortunately, as recounted in Chapter 9, VMMC had already decided to embark on a major improvement effort based upon Lean principles. So all the tools and knowledge, as well as the leadership's commitment to new ways of operating, were available to the planned clinic. It thus had the potential to become a model line within Virginia Mason—largely unconstrained by past decisions and not subject to a physical layout already determined.

With guidance from my consulting team, Dr. Hampson and his staff embarked upon their improvement journey. Some of the tools they used included the following:

- 3P
- RPIWs
- Standard work
- Focus on flow
- Pull-production system
- 5S workplace organization

Planning for Success with 3P

In 2002, to begin planning for the new facility, Dr. Hampson pulled together former patients, hospital administrators, and members of his staff into a 3P. This was an intensive, week-long workshop using modeling and timed simulation to determine the best layout for the hyperbaric chambers and the accompanying clinic.

Figure 10.4

Staff, led by John Black and Associates, using 3P to model the new hyperbaric facility.

Source: Virginia Mason Medical Center. Used with permission.

Initially, Hampson favored a 24-patient megachamber for the hyperbaric treatments. The head nurse leaned toward eight one-patient monochambers. The group modeled the competing designs on a large table using paper cups, plastic cookie-cutters, small tubes of paper, and other available items to mark out nursing stations, exam rooms, and other areas required for the patients. Then they sketched out the patient and staff flows within each model (Figure 10.4).

It soon became apparent that neither design minimized repetitious motion and patient/staff travel time within the clinic nor eliminated wasteful bottlenecks. Further modeling led the group to conclude that the optimal design for the space available would be to construct two eight-patient chambers side by side, with a common entry chamber between them. On each side of the entry chamber would be separate doors to enter each hyperbaric chamber. To enable staff to handle up to the maximum 16 patients without creating bottlenecks or requiring additional staff, the group decided to stagger the times of use for each chamber by one hour.

Asking *Why* Five Times Saves $2 Million

At this point, Dr. Hampson was contemplating the construction of a new building in a parking lot just east of the hospital to hold the new hyperbaric chamber module (which would be divided internally as discussed previously). It seemed there was no way to put the 46-foot-long, 10-foot-diameter module they'd designed into the existing hospital building. However, constructing a new building would impose an additional $2 million cost on the project.

This is where another Lean tool—asking why five times (5 whys process)—provided a cost-saving solution. As one might imagine, then VMMC President Mike Rona and CEO Gary Kaplan weren't thrilled with the idea of spending $2 million on a new building. Why couldn't Dr. Hampson put his module in the main hospital building? Rona was willing to make space available on the fourth floor by donating five scarcely used conference rooms and relocating the hospital library.

> **5 whys process:** Taiichi Ohno's practice of asking why five times whenever a problem was encountered in order to identify the root cause of the problem so that effective countermeasures could be developed and implemented

Dr. Hampson explained that the largest possible entry into the hospital (through the old basement garage) had only seven feet and three inches of clearance because of the hospital's main sewer pipe overhead. Rona and Kaplan persisted. Why couldn't Dr. Hampson find a way to bring the module in under the pipe?

At first it seemed obvious that one couldn't bring a structure with a 10-foot diameter through a garage with a seven-foot-three-inch clearance. But like many obvious obstacles, it soon disappeared beneath the weight of the kind of innovative thinking that Lean engenders. What if the module was constructed in pieces inside the hospital building— pieces no wider than seven feet that could be placed on their sides and pulled beneath the sewer pipe? That was the solution chosen and the 25,000-pound sections were slowly brought into the hospital and put together into the hyperbaric structure existing today. The result: $2 million was saved. And it didn't even take five whys.

An Environment By and For Patients

There's more to a medical facility than the staff and the physical lay-out. There's the ambience. What kind of feeling does one get from being there? This is where the patients on the planning team played the key role. They didn't want anything like the old hyperbaric department, which they viewed as cold and off-putting. Their desires would probably strike most healthcare patients as wishful thinking. The patients wanted

- a waiting room designed like a Starbucks lounge (including coffee bean designs on the furniture upholstery), with a television, for relatives and friends;
- male and female locker rooms, equivalent to those at an exercise club, for changing into scrubs and showering;
- semi-private nursing assessment stations;
- a comfortable gathering place to wait to enter the hyperbaric chambers;
- comfortable chairs inside each chamber;
- a way to keep the steel hyperbaric chamber from appearing so mechanical and intimidating; and
- warm, friendly colors throughout.

They got it all. According to the center's interior decorator, a patient going into the center for a hyperbaric treatment was like a sea turtle going from the woods to the ocean. So the waiting room for relatives and friends is decorated in soft greens and browns like a forest. The center floor is the color of sand near the entrance and the color of wet sand near the hyperbaric chamber. The chamber itself is a soft white and, as if in a submarine, fish are painted on the far wall outside the portholes. The ceiling is sky blue and rises in height as one approaches the chamber, shrinking the chamber's visual impact and bringing it down to human scale (Figure 10.5).

The patients' waiting area—the wait being as long or as short as patients make it—is called "the cabana." It is a pleasant, semicircu-

Figure 10.5

Virginia Mason's new hyperbaric chamber.

Source: Virginia Mason Medical Center. Used with permission.

lar area enclosed by a waist-high wall and contains comfortable chairs in a tropical motif. Adding to the cabana feeling are an aquarium and small, artificial coconut palms (Figure 10.6). At the patients' suggestion, a small refrigerator is located inside the cabana with bottled water to keep them hydrated in the hyperbaric chamber. The chairs inside the chambers are like the comfy recliners found in the business-class section of an airplane on an international flight.

Standardizing the Work

With a month to go until the opening of the new clinic, Dr. Hampson realized that although they had the space laid out and the

Figure 10.6

The patients' "cabana" at the new Center for Hyperbaric Medicine.

Source: Virginia Mason Medical Center. Used with permission.

ambience determined, no one had really thought about how every-one would work in the new facility. Questions ranged from basics as "Who would turn on the lights the first day?" to "What exactly was each person supposed to do in his or her shift?" Clinic staff knew how they'd operated in the old facility, but this was something new.

Their answer: an RPIW. To refresh your memory, this is a five-day *kaizen* event that achieves improvement in work flow while eliminating waste by empowering the people who do the work to make the changes.

One of the first decisions the group made was that standard work should be defined for every staff member, including doctors. For example, the steps and time involved in a new patient consult are specified for both nursing staff and the physician on a standard work sheet. This sheet is placed on a laminated card that fits in one's pocket and can be carried along as one performs one's duties (Figure 10.7).

Figure 10.7 Standard Work for New Patient Consult

	Quality Check	Safety Precaution	Standard WIP
	◇	✚	●

Notes:
This SWP replaces New Patient Consult SWP due to implementation of EZ Script

Who Must Adopt This Process: CHRN, CSR, MD
Describe the roles and types of work units

Takt Time: 255

GOAL: List key quality and lean targets

STEP (Add Quality, Safety or WIP symbols as needed)	OPERATOR (List role responsible for each task)	TASK DESCRIPTION	TOOLS/SUPPLIES REQUIRED (Fill in as needed to explain use of a specific tool or supply / Add photos if valuable to provide clear instructions)	CYCLE TIME (Add if converting to standard work)
1. ✚	CSR	Verifies the patient ID using "it takes two."	Patient label	
2.	CSR	Hands patient CHM history sheet if not already completed.	CHM history sheet	
3.	CSR	Receives completed history sheet.	CHM history sheet / IBM / Admit pack	
4.	CSR	Rooms patient, advises RN, passes history sheet, screening sheet, outside records, care plan. Puts billing sheet & orders in door pocket	CHM history sheet, Orange screening sheet, outside records, care plan, orders	
5.	CHRN	Enters room, greets patient, washes hands. Logs onto Cerner	Cerner terminal	
6. ◇	CHRN	Verifies the patient ID using "it takes two."		
7.	CHRN	Checks blood pressure and pulse. Checks weight	Cuff / Stethoscope / History Sheet / Scales	
8. ◇	CHRN	Reviews outside records. Reviews allergies, meds, pain. Updates Cerner PRN.	History sheets, Outside records, Orange screening sheet	
9.	CHRN	Logs off Cerner	Cerner terminal	
10.	CHRN	Puts history sheet in door pocket. Advises MD.	Admit screen / Care plan	
11.	MD	Picks up packet from door pocket.	Billing sheet, History sheet, Orders, Outside records	
12. ✚	MD	Enters room, greets patient, washes hands. Logs on to Cerner	Cerner terminal	
13. ◇	MD	Verifies the patient ID using "it takes two."	Patient label	
14. ◇	MD & CHRN	H & P by MD. Review outside records, Cerner records , allergies, meds.	Cerner terminal, History sheets, Outside records, Orange screening sheet, Orders	
15.	CHRN	Initiates Care Plan.	Care plan	
16. ✚	MD	Makes DX, PRN labs, orders TX plan, consents patient	Order	
17. ◇	CHRN	Tours patient, plans schedule, advises CSR of PRN labs.	Orders / Care plan / Orientation packet	
18.	CSR	Starts insurance preauth. PRN Labs.	IDX	
19.	MD	Dictates H & P, enters DX on billing sheet	Cerner terminal, History sheets, Outside records,	
20.	CSR	Reviews DX on billing sheet, enters on Cerner	Billing sheet / Cerner	

Version: Month/Year Oct 2006 | Approved by: List committee or leader | Sponsors: List executive (for organizational processes) or other leader(s)

Source: Virginia Mason Medical Center. Used with permission.

Patients Set Their Own Pace

To some degree, patient and staff flow had been determined during 3P mentioned earlier. However, the RPIW added an important enhancement: pull production. The idea here was that the patient would move through the system at her own pace, without being routed by clinic staff or held up by a lack of their availability. The use of *kanban* cards would enable this.

The laminated *kanban* cards, with letters large enough to be read at distance, bear the patient's last name, clinic and treatment numbers, and the date. Also, a large X is placed on the card if the patient needs to see the doctor after a hyperbaric treatment that day.

When a patient arrives at the clinic, the associated *kanban* card is in a clear plastic holder at the reception desk (Figure 10.8). Signing in is not needed. The patient takes the card and posts it on a large white board outside whichever chamber his treatment is scheduled for. This way, anyone can tell that the patient has arrived and in which chamber at what time he is scheduled to be treated.

The patient then goes to the male or female locker room and changes into scrubs. He then proceeds at his own rate to an assessment station to have his blood pressure read and to receive any other tests or preparation needed before entering the chamber. No nurse is posted at the station. That would represent waste, since it is used only for brief periods during the day. Instead, there's a call button at the station, which the patient pushes to call the nurse.

From here, the patient proceeds to the cabana to wait briefly before entering the assigned chamber with the others scheduled for the same time. Once finished, the patient either returns to the locker rooms, changes back into his clothes, returns the kanban card to the reception desk and departs, or proceeds to an examination room and posts his card on a Velcro holder outside the door announcing that he is ready to see the doctor, then goes inside and sits down. In this way, patients room themselves and call the physician service to them when they're ready.

Figure 10.8

Patient *kanban* card at Center for Hyperbaric Medicine reception counter.

Source: Virginia Mason Medical Center. Used with permission.

So, what we have is a patient-driven system that is highly effective from a flow standpoint. It minimizes use of staff and minimizes patient annoyance at being stuck at one or another treatment location—a win-win.

Clean and Clutter Free

Another Lean principle implemented was the 5S workplace organization. This is a visually oriented system for organizing the workplace; it includes keeping everything clean, neat, and in the proper location (clutter and hard-to-locate items are history). As explained previously, the five S's are sort, sweep, simplify, standardize, and self-discipline.

How was 5S applied to the Center for Hyperbaric Medicine? First, all supplies and documents are collected into similar batches and placed into cabinets or drawers clearly marked on the outside with their contents. Second, the clinic simplified the process for cleaning and restocking supplies in the chambers.

In the old method, nurses or technicians walked back and forth to the supply cabinet with dirty or clean items or for cleaning supplies. One idea from the RPIW was to provide two carts that staff could take into either chamber. One would have everything necessary for removing dirty items or for cleaning the chamber. The other would contain everything needed to restock it. Using the two carts cut the number of trips by a nurse from the supply cabinet and back down to two.

It's no surprise that a common comment by people first entering the center, according to Dr. Hampson, is, "Did you clean this place just for our visit?"

Dynamite Results

The new clinic has been open since early 2005. Here are some of the results from its first two years in operation.

- The staff workday has been collapsed from up to 14 hours to 8 hours, a 42 percent reduction. A second shift is not needed.
- The average number of patients per attendant in the hyperbaric chambers has increased from 2.4 in the old facility to 5.4 in the new one.
- Treatment hours are up 18 percent.
- Patient wait times have basically disappeared.
- Emergencies are treated without canceling routine treatments.
- Ergonomic complaints have been eliminated.
- $50,000 a year has been saved by eliminating ambulance transportation from the main hospital to the former facility across the street.
- Margins per patient are up 145 percent.

Although no hard data are available, patient and travel time in the new clinic have been dramatically reduced. More importantly, patient satisfaction appears extremely high from the feedback clinic staff has received. As for staff satisfaction, clinic workers are envied by those from other parts of the hospital; they frequently inquire about working in the hyperbaric center after visiting there.

How efficiently does the center run? According to Dr. Hampson, "the more patient hours increase, the higher the margin per hour."

Keeping the Ball Rolling

Isn't Dr. Hampson afraid of the backsliding so often seen after a major advance? Not at all. He has a staff committed to *kaizen* to keep him confident.

How is continuous incremental improvement maintained? In addition to staff commitment to Lean and the periodic RPIW, the clinic has implemented a waste-reduction program similar to a suggestion program (only more focused and one truly honored by management). Forms titled "My Everyday Lean Idea" are posted in areas where both patients and staff can access them.

The forms identify the seven kinds of waste (and hence improvement opportunities). Patients can only suggest their changes to staff, but staff members are encouraged to go ahead and put their ideas into practice (so long as other patients who would be affected agree) and report back the results. Improvements that work in practice are then institutionalized, and the innovating person or team is rewarded. It's hard to retreat when you're constantly advancing.

More on Virginia Mason's Everyday Lean Idea System

Virginia Mason's Everyday Lean Idea System was developed and piloted in 2003–2004, with a rollout to the organization beginning in earnest in 2005. It's designed to be the primary VMPS model to engage staff in improving their direct work with small, quick-to-do fixes that don't require substantial resources, time, or decision making.

The Everyday Lean Idea System is a departure from VMMC's former suggestion system, where staff sent their ideas to a central volunteer committee whose primary function was to search the organization for the right person(s) to evaluate the suggestion. Staff sometimes waited a year to hear back whether their ideas were accepted or rejected. Virginia Mason's new idea system, similar to other *kaizen* idea-system designs used by an increasing number of Japanese and Western companies, is intended to develop a take-action *kaizen* culture in which staff identify and fix small-scale problems in their immediate work areas.

Using a standard template, staff and leaders are guided through a five-step process in completing an everyday Lean idea:

- What's the problem and what types of waste is it causing?
- What's the idea to fix it?
- How can we test the idea?
- How do we know it worked?
- Will we implement the idea?

If staff have ideas about items outside their scope of control, they're encouraged to pass along the idea as feedback to the appropriate work team.

CHAPTER TAKEAWAYS

- By using 3P—and putting the patient first—a team in VMMC's cancer institute determined that creating space for a new facility in existing hospital space was better for patients than moving to space with a superior view in a building adjacent to the hospital.
- By using a variety of Lean principles and tools, the cancer institute was able to decrease patient lead time, increase the number of patients seen per therapist, and dramatically reduce staff walking distance.

- The cancer institute learned that small changes can lead to big improvements.
- Virginia Mason's Center for Hyperbaric Medicine is an excellent example of putting the patient first, with a facility designed substantially upon input from patients themselves.
- By using Lean tools such as 3P and the 5 whys process, center staff were able to save $2 million by locating the new center in existing hospital space rather than constructing a new facility.
- Patients proceed through the center at their own pace and obtain services as needed via a *kanban* system, saving time for both themselves and clinicians.
- Standard work cards help everyone know what is expected of them and the time required for each task.
- Some results: staff are working shorter hours while treating more patients, patient wait times have basically disappeared, and margins are up 145 percent.

CHAPTER 11

Lean Comes to
Park Nicollet Health Services

OVERVIEW: Implementing Lean at Park Nicollet Health Services involved similar steps as it did at Virginia Mason Medical Center, with the added challenge of first proving to Park Nicollet that Lean works *before* getting started. After three years, the results of applying Lean are impressive: Park Nicollet received the highest rating in 11 of 12 categories of the 2007 Health Care Quality Report by Minnesota Community Measurement, more than any other Minnesota healthcare provider (Whisnant 2004). Park Nicollet leaders share their thoughts on what they've learned in applying Lean, as well as the benefits they've seen.

PROVING LEAN WORKS

In early March 2003, I received a phone call from Mike Kaupa, then a senior vice president at Park Nicollet Health Services (PNHS) in Minneapolis, who'd been leading Six Sigma improvement efforts there. He said that he'd attended a week-long *kaizen* event at Virginia Mason in January, then added, "We've been doing Six Sigma for two years and have achieved modest results, but we want to talk to you about Lean."

On April 10, I flew to St. Paul to meet with Kaupa, Chief Medical Officer Sam Carlson, then Chief Operating Officer John Herman, and CEO David Wessner. Wessner wanted to know if I could integrate Six Sigma into Lean.

While Six Sigma tools can be used as part of taking the waste out of processes, I told him, "You have to put all of your improvement activities under one umbrella." I recommended he commit Park Nicollet to making that umbrella Lean. I told Wessner I could commit to applying Lean to PNHS, but I asked him, "Can you?"

Wessner said he wanted to see Lean work at PNHS before committing to full implementation, that is, he wanted us to provide him a test case. In my opinion, it's important to believe in Lean from the start, but I agreed to take his request to my consulting team and see if they would be willing to go along with it. As it turned out, they were.

To demonstrate the power of Lean at Park Nicollet, PNHS's endoscopy suite was chosen as the focus. At the time, it consisted of six rooms, serving an average of 30 to 35 patients a day. In one week of *kaizen*, an improvement team reorganized the rooms, adjusted patient scheduling, and implemented a new process for patient movement through the treatment process. The key result: with the same number of staff in the same space, the endoscopy suite now had the capacity to serve 72 patients a day—more than a 100 percent increase!

Team member Dr. George Logan, chief of gastroenterology in Park Nicollet's department of medicine, commented that "doctors were rightly worried that we'd ask them to work harder or faster, but we've improved the flow through the unit and turned over rooms more quickly without speeding up the actual procedures."

Wessner's statement to local healthcare journal *Minnesota Medicine* was, "Not only does Lean decrease costs, it also improves patient safety and creates capacity for future demand. We're excited about the work" (Whisnant 2004).

PROCEEDING FORWARD

A Name and Supporting Concepts

Wessner and his team decided to name their Lean effort the "Park Nicollet Health Support System." They defined it as "the systematic way we provide care that is continually more patient-centered, effective, efficient, safe, timely, and equitable."

Park Nicollet also developed some supporting concepts.

- Mission: To care for and support the health, healing, and learning of those we serve
- Values: Excellence, caring, stewardship, joy, and learning
- Vision: Everyone caring, every day, creating optimal health and greater value with the individuals we serve
- Value = Patient-centered outcomes and experience ÷ Price and Time

Ensuring Leader Involvement

From the beginning, it was clear that Park Nicollet needed to begin establishing the infrastructure to support the internal management system that would drive and sustain Lean. This would require a paradigm shift, especially when it came to the "hands on" involvement of leaders. In this regard, the contract between PNHS and the consulting firm contains the following language regarding certifying Lean leaders at Park Nicollet:

- Construct value-stream maps to identify *kaizen* opportunities.
- Complete three-day training of top 50 leaders.
- Complete three-day intensive seminar, with learning and presenting the 24 improvement modules (see Chapter 6, Building *Kaizen* Leaders).

- Complete two workshops as participant.
- Complete two workshops as a sub-team leader.
- Complete two workshops as a team leader.
- Lead several workshops under consultant's guidance.
- Attend "Wash Your Hands" training at Genie-Terex in Redmond, Washington.
- Attend Japan *gemba kaizen* (shop-floor education).

This was asking for a significant time commitment from everyone, starting with Wessner: 100 percent of each leader's time for "week minus three" in preparing for their first *kaizen* event, 50 percent for "week minus two," 25 percent for "week minus one," and 100 percent for the week of the workshop. But the goal had to be that *kaizen* would become Park Nicollet's way of doing business, its way of life.

Implementing Lean Is Not a Cake Walk

Even with a sense of urgency, implementing Lean would require a long-term commitment. The system exposes waste mercilessly, and, as the waste waterline goes down, resistance to change goes up. People must be prepared to abandon familiar and long-standing practices. Park Nicollet leaders had to be ready to clear away obstacles and to implement and maintain the system. Mid-level managers had to provide shop-floor leadership in putting Lean concepts into practice. This message had to be clear to PNHS leaders before we got started.

On July 31, 2003, a five-year contract was signed between Park Nicollet and John Black and Associates, and we embarked on an aggressive Lean implementation schedule that today includes deploying Japanese consultants as well. On March 20, 2007, we signed an extension to 2010. This demonstrates that Lean truly has come to healthcare.

Result from Lean's Implementation at Park Nicollet

Table 11.1 shows the impressive results PNHS has achieved since beginning Lean implementation in 2004.

Table 11.1 Statistical Results of Lean Implementation at Park Nicollet

Space, in square feet, reduced and available for alternate use	16,512
Miles cut from total distance staff walks each day	265
Miles cut from total distance patients walk each day	2.3
Miles cut from total distance parts (i.e., lab letters and radiology results) travel each day	43.6
Number of surgical instruments no longer processed each month	79,530
Number of excess inventory items eliminated	839,500
Value of eliminated inventory items	$662,135
Number of defects eliminated each day	4,788
Number of FTEs redeployed	18
Average percent difference in output per FTE*	115
Number of hours patients or staff no longer wait in lead time each day	16,290
Number of minutes staff no longer spend in setup each day	98
Number of hours staff no longer waste in cycle time each day	631
Number of additional patients who can be seen each day due to increased capacity	229.4

* 2006 number includes FTEs impacted by 7 RPIW teams with a percentage productivity range of 11–62;
2005 number includes FTEs impacted by 7 RPIW teams with a percentage productivity range of 5–240;
2004 number includes FTEs impacted by 13 RPIW teams with a percentage productivity range of 3–60.

In Chapter 12, you'll learn about some of the specific model lines at Park Nicollet and the successes they've achieved. For the rest of this chapter, PNHS's leaders will share their trials and triumphs in implementing Lean, with you, the reader, hopefully becoming a budding Lean believer.

IN THEIR OWN WORDS

Recognizing the Need for Change and the Power of Lean

CEO David Wessner: From my days at Duke University as a graduate student, I had been aware of how much waste and inconsistency of care existed within the American heathcare system. I even wrote my thesis about applying a "systems approach" to inpatient care.

We'd looked at Six Sigma, but it takes people out of the work environment to solve a problem whereas Lean brings people to the work environment to solve it. Also, the pace is totally different. What really convinced me to go ahead with Lean, though, was when John Black came to Park Nicollet and told me that, through Lean, we could double the capacity of our endoscopy operation without adding more space.

To my knowledge, Lean is the only management system robust enough to handle the complexity of healthcare. However, that doesn't mean it's an easy application. You have to work hard at it.

Benefits of Lean to Park Nicollet

Wessner: Without getting into all the statistics, Lean has provided a lot of improvement in terms of cutting waste, increasing patient volume, reducing inventory, enhancing safety, and boosting quality of care. More than that, it's given us greater responsiveness in fixing problems and in adjusting to change. We've performed about 300 Lean projects so far aimed at improving what we do.

We've benefited and learned from every one of them to a greater or lesser extent.

COO Mike Kaupa: One of the most important benefits of Lean has been the application of a common vocabulary and common tools for improving our operations that extends across professional and other boundaries. This "common denominator" is very powerful and is helping us develop "organizational fitness." By that, I mean getting rid of "fat" (i.e., waste). Lean also is helping with another aspect of fitness, and that's the ability to rapidly adjust to change.

One of our greatest successes has been with *kanban* and just-in-time inventory. Especially at our hospital, we've achieved dramatic reductions in supplies and inventory. Previously, we had to throw away some of our supplies because their expiration date had gone by. A major change in mind-set is that our staff has come to understand the difference between "batch" and "one-piece flow"—for example, with lab results or charge tickets—and have realized that one-piece flow is often the better way to go.

Our repeat patients are noticing that we're providing greater value to them. One way is through quicker, more reliable visits. We've especially reduced patient lead time—the time it takes for a patient to receive treatment and go home—in our orthopedic clinic. Another way we're providing greater value is through price reductions we've been able to achieve for some services.

CMO Sam Carlson: Lean has provided a common language so that most of us are comfortable in describing our challenges for access in terms of *takt* time and lead time, looking for the seven wastes and calling them out, understanding work-in-process in describing flow problems, and using the word *kaizen* without explaining what it means. We've learned the value of making our problems visible and applying daily management at the local team level. Standardized rooming processes across primary care and many specialty care areas has certainly reduced defects, and we're reconciling lab results much more accurately now. Our GI endoscopy unit flows very well now, with very little waiting for patients or physicians, with reduced walking by our nursing staff. All our new facilities have gone through 3P and, as a result, are much more efficiently designed than in the past.

Progress in Building the Infrastructure

Wessner: We've gotten a lot done in getting people trained. People are learning the tools and adopting a common language of improvement. As of the early summer of 2007, we've certified approximately 100 of our staff as "Lean leaders," with another 100 in the certification pipeline. I expect our managers to lead the Lean effort, whether or not they've been certified.

Basically, what Lean provides is an effective, organization-wide approach to improving what we do into the future. I would say our staff is pretty much on board in understanding the value of Lean and accepting it as our common management system.

Gary Larson, vice president, *Kaizen* Promotion Office: Our goal is to have 1 percent of our workforce dedicated to *kaizen*. We are close to that now, with nearly 60 people assigned full-time to Lean implementation. Some of these people report to me; most report to service-line leaders. In the overall KPO, we have 14 people, including four "replication specialists" and five "lead *kaizen* specialists."

We've developed a "*kaizen* career ladder," so people can advance in their careers by focusing on Lean implementation. We have *kaizen* specialist levels 1 and 2 (level 2 being "replication specialists"), *kaizen* lead specialists, *kaizen* directors, and a KPO vice president. Within the regular career paths, being *kaizen* certified is important to becoming a director or vice president.

We've established *Kaizen* Operation Teams in each of our five major service lines—surgery, primary care, hospital inpatient, medical subspecialties, and corporate services (e.g., finance, materials, human resources, facilities). These KOTs report to me on a dotted-line basis and to the service-line leaders on a direct basis.

Kaupa: In terms of depth, we're of course deeper in the model service lines we started four years ago than ones started more recently.

Putting the Patient First

Wessner: Our people understood the importance of focusing on the patient long before Lean. We've reinforced that focus through a new vision statement which replaces the word "service" with "care." This adds the emotional element involved. However, before Lean, I don't think our employees adequately understood the connection between improving our processes and efficiency and the notion of caring. To really care for our patients, we have to go beyond individual actions.

Overcoming Obstacles and Resistance

Wessner: A particular challenge we in healthcare have to deal with is that when you're caring for patients—sometimes on a 24-hour basis as in inpatient or surgery—it's hard to break out the time you need to focus on improvement efforts. Implementing Lean initially increases the amount of work people have to do, so if they don't see that they're working on what they view as immediate problems, they can ease up on Lean implementation. That's why it's important to align Lean with what people view as the most urgent problems. It's also important to lay the groundwork for concentrated Lean improvement projects (e.g., RPIWs) by improving daily management, for example, by first establishing standard work.

Another way we combat resistance is by continually publicizing our Lean successes through e-mail messages, visuals such as charts in visibility rooms, and other means. As well, leadership continually reinforces through our management structure the need to focus on Lean, making it the normal way our work gets done. Another powerful motivator is letting people know that promotion to higher levels of leadership requires knowledge of Lean and use of its processes and tools.

Kaupa: Another obstacle, unlike the situation Toyota and many other Japanese companies faced after World War II, is that we're not coming from a place of scarcity in the United States. We don't have that particular pressure to psychologically prepare us to squeeze the most we can from our resources. And, to be honest, our industry thus far hasn't suffered from the kind of competitive pressures that other industries face. We don't have the scenario of a hospital down the street offering surgeries at half price, for example.

I think people are getting on board. To a large extent, the results speak for themselves. Clinicians, in varying degrees and levels within the organization, are seeing their work getting easier through Lean improvements. Another way we're bringing people on board—in addition to the training—is by selecting people for leadership based on their Lean experience and commitment. We're also challenging each other to model the behaviors we expect. Finally, of course, we're holding people responsible for their Lean results. For example, standard work is standard work; leaders either produce it or they don't.

Carlson: Many physicians and support staff held the view that manufacturing and healthcare were so different that similar tools couldn't be applied, and we've heard the statement "we're not making cars here" many times. We've had some deliberate attempts to undermine the results, and those are dealt with by respectful private conversations.

Larson: There's still work to be done to get people to understand the connection between Lean and our mission. An effective way of doing this is by getting people involved in RPIWs. Exposure to Lean, seeing that it's effective in making significant improvements, usually converts the participants. So far, about 1,500 of our 8,000 employees have been involved. We've created some real zealots for Lean this way.

The Role of Leadership

Wessner: I have to be the head cheerleader and the head expectation setter. I have to stay committed to Lean, demonstrably so, keep promoting its benefits, and demand that people stick with it.

Kaupa: My role is to set expectations and model the change we want. I have to make sure that no one gets the sense that Lean is optional. I also walk the floors to observe for myself how things are going, providing input where appropriate.

There are three things we as leaders must do:

1. *Persevere.* We have to remember we're on a 20-year journey.
2. *Be courageous.* We can't give in to skepticism and we have to be willing to not be popular.
3. *Work every day on "shaping the culture."* The goal is to make Lean our everyday way of operating.

Larson: My role is to help build the Lean infrastructure and Lean skill sets we need, and to make sure we're applying Lean consistently across the organization. That means stubbornly sticking with the established *kaizen* tools. Creativity needs to be focused on improving our processes, not the *kaizen* tools. I also need to help make sure all of our service lines are aligned and pulling together in this effort.

My role also requires me to be a motivator and cheerleader. I have to paint a picture, a vision, of where we need to go. For me, this is getting to the quality and service levels some other industries provide their customers—for example, really good financial institutions.

Beyond that, I have to help people understand that Lean is a long-term commitment that extends indefinitely into the future—that benefits will grow and accumulate over time. This means I have to spend a lot of time talking to people who are doing the work and reinforcing the value of their efforts. Obviously, I have to have a passion for improvement and, also, for Lean as the way to the improvement.

Looking Ahead

Wessner: We still haven't improved flow across the organization. We don't yet know how increased demand in one service line affects demand in another. We need to move from point improvements to line improvements, from improving a process in one department or part of a department, to leveling production across departments and the entire system … and making standard operations in one part of the organization standard work throughout the organization.

Perhaps the most important challenge in the near term is really creating quality teamwork. Team members have to understand their Lean roles as a team and not just as individuals. For example, "How do we visualize our team goals and work on them daily?" This task is made more difficult by the fact that teams may reconfigure during the day depending on the cases that present themselves or other tasks that need to be done, and teams change by shift.

Kaupa: One challenge is that we have no measure of true demand. All we find is that as we add capacity, the queue just gets backfilled, sort of like "if you build it, they will come." It seems the demand is endless.

Ex Post Facto

Carlson: We were probably understaffed earlier, and so when a team would complete their efforts and move on, improvements would sometimes fade away, since there was no trained person to maintain them. We're in a much better spot now. We may also have focused on too much of a centralized approach; keeping the ownership more at the local care-team level might have allowed more progress in some areas.

Wessner: If I could start over again from scratch in implementing Lean, I would require that we improve daily management in certain areas before embarking on RPIWs—get the team priorities set and standard work established first. Doing so helps sustain the gains of the RPIWs.

CHAPTER TAKEAWAYS

- Six Sigma was not working for Park Nicollet Health Services, so CEO David Wessner requested a test of Lean in PNHS's endoscopy suite in early 2003. In one week of *kaizen*, a team was able to increase patient throughput by more than 100 percent.
- In July 2003, Wessner signed a five-year consulting contract with John Black and Associates to implement Lean (since extended to 2010).
- After a few bumps along the way, PNHS is now achieving impressive results such as reduced space requirements and patient/staff walking distance, excess inventory eliminated (with consequent cost savings), and dramatic increases in staff output.
- PNHS leaders discussed their Lean learnings in their own words in ways that will benefit the reader.

REFERENCE

Whisnant, R. 2004. "Lean Production at Park Nicollet." *Minnesota Medicine* 87 (2): 9.

CHAPTER 12

Park Nicollet Health Services Case Studies

OVERVIEW: The case studies in this chapter further demonstrate the power of Lean in enhancing patient flow, reducing defects, and achieving cost savings. Some of the improvements applied include self-rooming, onsite blood testing, and more efficient facility design. A careful analysis of instrument usage by Park Nicollet surgeons enabled the elimination of excess inventory.

PRIMARY CARE

Primary care, the area of patient care delivery that treats patients not requiring specialty care, is a major component of any healthcare system. This is where the majority of the medical system's customers (patients) interact with it and its personnel.

Park Nicollet's primary care service line maintains twenty primary care clinics, including six urgent care clinics in Minneapolis and its western suburbs. Each year, approximately one million patients visit these clinics for checkups or treatment.

For the past two years, Lean leaders in the primary care service line have focused on improving the way patients move through their clinics (rooming) and ensuring timely lab results, as well as increasing the percentage of patients with optimally managed diabetes.

Standard Rooming

Patients who come to one of PNHS's primary care clinics are escorted to the exam room by a nurse. There, the nurse collects information from the patient, such as the reason for the patient's visit, and measures vital signs, including blood pressure and temperature. This is known as the *patient rooming process.*

Prior to the implementation of Lean, nurses' rooming methods differed. Patients were greeted in a variety of ways. There was no clear standard for what data should be collected and in what order. As a result, the clinician did not always know what data already had been collected and often repeated the same questions the nurse had already asked the patient. The result of the inconsistent rooming was a longer lead time for the overall patient visit and rework in the collection of patient data. This problem was related to, and compounded by, a lack of consistency in visit planning (planning in advance for patient requirements).

Seven RPIWs spanning two years culminated in a full-scale roll-out to establish and perfect standard work for patient rooming in primary care. A variety of leaders were identified to direct and assist with these projects, with a heavy emphasis on nursing involvement. Three weeks of preparation occurred prior to the RPIW week. Highlights of the seven projects include the following:

- Pre-service patient lead time was reduced by 31.8 percent at three major targeted sites.
- Patient rooming time, which initially bore an inverse relationship to the number of defects, experienced an overall reduction of 10 percent—from 7:17 minutes to 6:30 minutes.
- Room change-over time decreased from 45 seconds to 15 seconds, a reduction of 67 percent.

- The overall rooming defect rate went from 89 percent to 9 percent across 20 primary care clinic locations. (The "defects" generally didn't affect patient health or safety, but represented rework by the physician in obtaining data that nurses or others hadn't yet provided the physician, e.g., vital signs or lab results.)
- By printing lab results ("lab letters") directly to individual departments electronically at each clinic site, the manual driving of reports to sites was cut from 62,120 miles a year to zero (100 percent) and the lead time for the patient to obtain lab results from 240 hours to 5 (98 percent).
- Patient self-rooming at the Park Nicollet Clinic–Chanhassen facility enabled the nurse there to cut walking distance needed to serve each patient from 659 feet to 232 feet, a 65 percent reduction. (Incoming patients are given a color-coded card, representing an area of the clinic, with their name and a number on it that directs them to the correct room for treatment. The patient's location is tracked through a computer application and each stage of the clinic visit is advanced by the medical personnel interacting with the patient.)
- Also, by establishing a quick-check process at one urgent care clinic (identifying patients with specific, simpler treatment needs and moving them through a faster track of treatment), lead time for all patients was reduced from 56 minutes to 32 minutes—a 43 percent reduction. This process will be rolled out to the other five urgent care clinics by the end of 2007.
- Patient satisfaction scores increased by 5 percent in both primary care and urgent care, partly through a new process of tapping available primary care appointment slots (due to cancellations) for overflow urgent care demand.

Both Dr. Beth Hartquist, chief of primary care, and Bill Kenney, senior vice president of primary care, agree that many of the improvements made were common sense and simple in concept, thought not always easy to implement. "So far as rooming is concerned, one of our chief goals is producing the 'fully prepared patient' for the clinician," says Kenney. "What we're attempting to eliminate is incomplete information being provided to the clinician."

Another element in producing the fully prepared patient is *visit planning* by the nurse. This entails knowing what is needed during each particular patient's medical visit and making sure that those needs are met when the patient meets the clinician. Standard work has eliminated the previous inconsistency in visit planning.

Managing Patients with Type II Diabetes

Another major area of emphasis for Park Nicollet's primary care service line is the management of its 9,000 Type II diabetes patients. The main target is to increase the percentage of patients receiving optimally managed care according to the Minnesota Community Measurement Project (MCMP), a nonprofit entity dedicated to improving the quality of healthcare in Minnesota. The standards measure a patient's progress in five areas: A1C (blood sugar), blood pressure, cholesterol (LDL), alcohol use, and tobacco use.

In order to help patients move into the category of "optimally managed," three areas were identified as follows:

1. *Preparation for the chronic disease visit:* Patients with chronic diseases typically have many specific needs that require accurate and timely action and follow-up. PNHS lacked standard work to prepare patients for the visit.
2. *Clinician visit with next-visit setup:* PNHS did not have uniform tools or standard work (electronic or paper) to prepare for ongoing chronic disease visits or planned laboratory tests.
3. *Diabetes registry usage:* There was no standard use of the diabetes registry, which was compounded by a lack of understanding of who can use the registry. The registry tracks needed care versus care delivered for diabetes patients.

Four RPIWs were conducted over a six-month period to establish and perfect a uniform process for visit planning and population management for Type II diabetes patients. These RPIWs focused on better visit planning, including speeding the time from the patient's blood draw to having the results available for the physician to discuss with the patient during the face-to-face visit.

"The process at the time consisted of us drawing the patient's blood *after* the doctor visit," says Dr. Hartquist. "The samples were sent to a central lab for testing, the results placed in large batches and returned to us days later, and then we had to spend a great deal of time calling patients and arranging for the clinician to discuss results with them. This could take many calls and we might never connect. The process was staff intensive, time consuming, and relatively ineffective."

The solution: Park Nicollet invested in six smaller, handheld blood-testing devices and installed one in each laboratory at six of its sites. The process, developed through value-stream mapping, is to have the patient arrive a half-hour prior to the physician appointment and get blood drawn then. The sample is processed immediately via the onsite testing machine and the clinician has the results in hand when the patient arrives. In this way, the clinician has the information necessary to accurately advise the patient on how to obtain optimal health results. Also, the lead time from patient blood draw to result notification has been cut 99 percent, from an average of six days and five hours to 39 minutes.

A related issue was the simple lack of any visit-planning process, including reviewing patient information on the diabetes registry to see whether the patient had been receiving recommended checkups and the corresponding results. Without this reference, the clinician had little way of knowing whether a new patient was progressing or regressing in terms of the five health measures on the MCMP or whether the patient was following the recommended treatment regime. The solution here was simply to implement a standard process for visit planning, including mandatory reference to the diabetes registry.

"Prior to this effort," says Dr. Hartquist, "we didn't know if results were being reviewed with patients and whether important tests were being missed. Now, every order for treatment is written on a specific form that makes sure all lab results have been performed and results communicated to the patient. This is extremely important for meeting the 'results reconciliation' requirements of the Joint Commission, which accredits healthcare facilities."

This work has resulted in improvement in the percentage of patients receiving optimally managed care from 6 percent to 16 percent. Park Nicollet estimates that if it were able to optimize care for its 9,000 Type II diabetes patients, they would experience 183 fewer serious events (e.g., stroke or amputation). Furthermore, the Centers for Disease Control and Prevention estimates that controlling diabetes patients to near non-diabetes status would cut their annual medical costs by more than 80 percent (from $13,240 to $2,560).

Primary Care's Lean Experience to Date

According to Dr. Hartquist, primary care has spent the last two years "addressing basic infrastructure issues," including setting up a KOT and involving a number of physicians and nurses in Lean certification. Still, she admits that there was a certain amount of resistance to Lean at first. "There's a strong professional culture that sometimes competes with the needs of the organization. Physicians are still not trusting of a system that requires giving up some autonomy."

"One of our obstacles in implementing Lean has been that we're spread out over many sites across a large geography," adds Kenney. "There's a lot of grassroots talk about what worked and what didn't. Our experience is that bad news travels fast; good news much more slowly."

One of the best ways to focus on what's being accomplished, they believe, is through what they call "visual management boards." These are now in place in every clinic. The expectation is that clinic leadership review them twice a day to go over the day's targeted activities. They concede, however, that the boards have received mixed reviews so far. They believe this is partly due to the wide variation in clinic size and staffing.

Overall, they're both very optimistic about the future. "We're now well positioned to really improve quality," says Dr. Hartquist. "Our diabetes work shows the promise."

"It's really exciting," adds Kenny. "It's fun."

And it pays off. Due to the primary clinics' improved quality, PNHS received $2.5 million in "pay for performance" bonuses from major insurance companies in 2006.

MEDICAL SUBSPECIALTIES

Park Nicollet maintains one of the largest multispecialty clinics in the United States, providing care in 45 medical and surgical specialties. The medical subspecialties service line consists of 21 departments made up of 750 employees. Two of the departments where significant Lean work has occurred are the gastroenterology (GI) department and the endoscopic procedure center. These two organizations are now housed at PNHS's new digestive and endoscopic procedure center—in a way "a house that Lean built." Here's how they got there.

In 2003, the endoscopic procedure center and the GI clinic were both staffed by the same practicing group of five clinicians; however, they were physically located at separate sites. An average of 30 endoscopic procedures were performed per day. Demand for some endoscopic procedures, especially screening colonoscopies, was increasing as a result of changing patient demographics (aging of the large baby-boom cohort), as well as changing clinical standards (e.g., national medical organizations recommending screening colonoscopies rather than sigmoidoscopies for many patients).

This was one of the reasons Park Nicollet senior leaders identified the endoscopy center as a likely candidate to benefit from the application of Lean. It became the first learning laboratory for

PNHS. Over the next four years, a series of 12 RPIWs were conducted. As well, other Lean tools were applied to the challenge of better handling growing demand, including the use of 3P to design the new digestive and endoscopic procedure center, which opened in February of 2007.

Enhancing Patient Flow

"When we began our Lean journey, we believed we'd maxed out our endoscopy department's capacity," says Joan Sandstrom, vice president for medical subspecialties. "Our five GI physicians were performing 30 to 35 procedures a day and we believed we couldn't fit any more physicians into the current space and therefore couldn't perform any additional procedures per day."

Medical subspecialties aimed its first RPIW squarely at the issue of improving patient flow and throughput on the day of service. Their goals were as follows:

- increase the number of clinicians without adding facilities,
- increase the number of procedures performed per day,
- create a balanced schedule to utilize staff and space at the optimum level,
- document standard work processes for each role, and
- decrease walking for nurses and other endoscopy staff.

The initial approach taken was to create a pull system with the following elements:

- *Use cascade scheduling.* This entails staggering the times when patients were scheduled for treatment to avoid bottlenecks.
- *Develop a patient-tracking system.* Lean teachings encourage the creation of manual and paper processes before moving to anything electronic, so a manual process of laminated cards with numbers on them was created as a patient-tracking system. At

check-in, each patient was assigned a number. This number, in the form of the laminated card, followed the patients as they moved from room to room. As patients arrived at each room, staff would place the card in a plastic holder outside the door. This enabled staff to quickly and easily identify where a patient was in the process, while maintaining confidentiality by not revealing patient names. Next, nurses who had previously worked only in one portion of the process such as pre-assessment, followed the patient through the procedure, with the charge nurse acting as the "air traffic controller," coordinating assignments of these nurses from an "on-deck" status to receiving an assignment.

- *Use a light system (*andon*) to indicate when a room would be available.* This innovative use of *andon* let staff know when a patient in a room was within 12 minutes of procedure completion. Staff then knew to pull the next patient into the process, rather than pushing the patient into the process after the procedure room was already emptied.

- *Apply standard work to patient setup.* This involves a nurse reviewing with the patient all pertinent information including physical status, medications, bowel preparation, etc., to ensure he is adequately prepared for his procedure (or identify a defect that would preclude the patient from undergoing the procedure). One step in the pre-assessment process is to start an IV in the patient. This requires five items. An IV kit was developed with all five items in it, so that the nurse could easily find all the items required.

Among the results of this first RPIW were the reduction of nurse walking distance per patient by 50 percent (from 720 feet to 360) and the reduction of nurse set-up time by 40 percent (from 11:41 to 7 minutes). Perhaps most importantly, day-of-service patient lead time was cut from approximately two hours to 90 minutes. More procedures could now be performed in a day in the same space with the same doctors. The flow improvements allowed for the addition of more physicians, which in turn increased the average volume to approximately 42 procedures per day.

A subsequent, related RPIW rearranged *how* patients moved through the department. One improvement was having patients' clothes travel with them from room to room, so they didn't have to return to the same room where they changed into treatment garb to change back into their normal wear. This prevented backups that had previously occurred when patients changing to leave the facility needed to use the same rooms as people just changing into hospital wear.

"A major opportunity lay in redesigning the 'hand-offs' of patients," says Dr. Michael Feldman, chief of medical subspecialties. "This included how they were scheduled, where they changed clothes, room changeover, when they moved to recovery, and more. Through greater coordination, we were able to start maximizing everyone's time."

Adds Sandstrom: "We learned it's better to move things to the patient than the patient to things."

Over time, other RPIWs increased patient flow more. In January 2004, an RPIW addressed supply storage and the role of the health unit coordinator (HUC), who performs such functions as registering patients, answering the phones, and preparing necessary paperwork. By changing paperwork preparation from being performed in several large batches to one-piece flow, the HUC was able to reduce the paperwork-preparation cycle time per patient from 19 minutes to 12:10.

While improving storage supply might seem unrelated to flow, it is not. Using the 5S process to reduce clutter and better organize supplies in the supply room, staff no longer wasted time looking for supplies that were not where they expected them or were poorly labeled. At the same time, inventory was reduced by thousands of dollars—$7,285 to be exact—by analyzing what supplies were required and what minimal amounts (or par levels) of each supply are necessary. Continued flow improvements allowed the endoscopy department to continue to add physicians, which enabled it to add capacity to the practice and increase the number of average procedures performed per day to 46.

In July of 2004, an RPIW was again conducted to look at productivity and procedure volume. One difficulty the department faced was that a larger number of procedures were scheduled to occur in the morning than in the afternoon. This meant that the physicians, support staff, and facility did not have a level workload, so clinicians found it necessary to work very hard in the morning hours and then face a less busy afternoon. Therefore, this RPIW aimed at schedule changes that could level work across the day (*heijunka.*)

Using an architect's drawing of the department, different colored Legos® representing various actors and resources (patients, physicians, nurses, technicians, and equipment), and a stopwatch to count cycle times, the team modeled a scenario of six doctors and 65 procedures per day. Through this exercise, the team determined that the procedure capacity of the endoscopy department, as then constituted, was 65 procedures per day with a leveled schedule. However, this leveled schedule could not be implemented in the existing facility as it would have disadvantaged care in the GI clinic.

A New Facility

As demand for endoscopic procedures kept climbing, it became more and more apparent that a new facility was needed. In July of 2004, 3P was conducted to design a single-location digestive center that would combine the current and future needed patient services for both the endoscopy department and the GI clinic, as well as the square-footage space needs for the new facility.

However, at the time of this 3P, there was no location available within Methodist Hospital to accommodate a center of the size needed. So Park Nicollet leaders decided to delay construction of a new digestive center until construction of a planned new building— one that would already contain adequate space for the digestive center—was completed. This would take another 18 months.

To provide a bridge to the future—and accommodate increasing procedure volumes from a staff of now seven GI physicians—a small, "bridge" endoscopic suite was built. Many of the Lean learnings from previous *kaizen* events were included in the design of this small unit, which consisted of five multi-use, pre- and post-procedure rooms, two procedure rooms, a U-shaped scope cleaning room, and a storage room.

A second 3P was conducted in February of 2006. By carefully analyzing the demographics and anticipated GI health needs of the PNHS market area—and by again locating Lego blocks on floor plans and using a stopwatch for cycle times—the team planned patient flow and facility needs within the newly constructed building.

The resulting design included a total of four pods—one for the GI clinic practice and three for endoscopic procedures. Of the latter, two were slated to be opened initially and a third would be added as volume dictated. Each endoscopy pod consisted of seven procedure rooms and six recovery rooms. (It was clear from 3P that creating smaller work pods and placing a smaller number of procedure rooms, recovery rooms, and nurses' stations near each other would save many steps for staff and physicians.) The GI clinic pod was designed with seven exam rooms. The complete facility has space for up to 19 clinicians and support staff.

With the opening of the new facility, capacity has now increased to 80 procedures per day. The facility was designed to support growing volumes through 2025. At full staffing of 19 GI physicians, with corresponding capacity and efficiency, the center will be able to accommodate up to 160 endoscopic procedures and 60 clinic visits per day.

Another RPIW, in April of 2006, focused on increasing the efficiency of scheduling the growing number of procedures. This RPIW created a new process that decreased the cycle time to schedule an endoscopic procedure, decreased errors and rework in the scheduling process, and created a method to shrink the backlog of approximately 3,500 unscheduled procedure requests. By replacing the previous paper-based scheduling process with a person-to-person, phone-call system, cycle time for schedulers was reduced from more than 15 minutes to just over 5. This has enabled schedulers to eliminate the backlog of unscheduled procedure requests in the new center. It also has helped reduce errors in paperwork, particularly lost paperwork.

As well, better designed space in the new facility has reduced patient walking distance from 2,482 feet to 1,216, a 51 percent improvement.

Where Is My Biopsy Report?

One of the things that frustrated patients and sometimes delayed treatment was the amount of time it took for endoscopy patients to receive the results of a biopsy. In February of 2006, an RPIW set goals of decreasing the lead time from specimen collection to the patient receiving results by 50 percent, while also increasing regulatory-agency compliance regarding documentation of orders for follow-up testing and visits.

Under the pre-RPIW process, biopsy information was mailed from the endosocpy department to the GI clinic and "parked" there until the physicians were in the clinic to review the report and generate a letter to each patient. (At the time of the RPIW, the endoscopy department and GI clinic were separated by a mile.) By keeping the biopsy results in the endoscopy department and developing an electronic template for the generation of patient-result letters, a big delay was removed. The lead time from specimen collection to results to patient was reduced by 50 percent (from 14 to 7 days) and the cycle time per physician per patient-result letter was decreased from 12:32 to 2:45, a 78 percent decrease. Also, by developing and monitoring standard work for documentation of orders, regulatory compliance for this documentation increased from 20 percent to 100 percent.

And There's More

Other RPIWs accomplished the following:

- *June 2006.* Implementing a 2-bin, or *kanban*, ordering and restocking system in endoscopy cut supply inventory from 5,978 items to 3,497, a 41 percent reduction.

- *October 2006.* Frontline staff from GI and endsocopy were cross-trained to perform the functions needed by both departments.
- *November 2006.* Kitted supplies for bronchoscopy procedures reduced inventory from 30 individual items that would need to be collected to 11, and lowered space needed for supplies from 970 square feet to 595. Improved load leveling of bronchoscopies and creation of new standard work for respiratory therapists and assisting nurses reduced cycle time for the respiratory therapist from 90 minutes to 42.
- *December 2006.* The Lean tool of "autonomous maintenance" resulted in new endoscope cleaning and storage procedures that are keeping the expensive endoscopes safe from damage. All endoscopy equipment has been cataloged and entered into a computerized preventive maintenance database that will alert maintenance, bio-med, and information technology staff when to perform preventive maintenance. This is expected to significantly decrease repair costs in the new digestive center.

Dr. Feldman and Sandstrom are very enthusiastic about the gains from Lean. They admit there was some initial resistance from clinicians who feared Lean would mechanize medical care. Their message over and over was that by reducing the waste in processes, particularly those that are not direct patient care activities, doctors and nurses can *increase* the time available for personal attention to patients. They also discovered that anxiety about RPIWs and the changes they might bring could be overcome by meeting with the department involved beginning 10 weeks prior to an RPIW and "letting them know what's coming," as well as by inviting their input regarding what problems and processes they would like the RPIW to focus on. Additional meetings also occur four weeks and one week prior to the RPIW—and more often if necessary to ensure departmental engagement and success.

Skeptics are rarer these days. The successful recruitment of gastroenterologists, who are in high demand at present, has enabled endoscopy procedures to increase to the previously mentioned 80 per day, and the number of clinic visits has risen as well. However, the digestive center is still struggling to meet rising demand.

"Although we now have a total of nine gastroenterologists, these specialists are retiring faster than they're coming out of fellowship programs," Dr. Feldman says. "Therefore, to successfully recruit, we must assist in creating environments and processes in which they can practice as efficiently and effectively as possible."

Lean is helping Park Nicollet's medical subspecialties do just that.

SURGICAL SERVICES: CASE CART STANDARIZATION

Approximately 17,000 surgeries were performed in 2006 at PNHS's Methodist Hospital. Each surgery requires multiple instrument trays on several carts with potentially hundreds of instruments and myriad supplies, from drapes to sutures. Factor in surgeon preference and the variation between similar cases is staggering, making standardization a complex and challenging undertaking.

"More often than not," says Dr. Steven M. Connelly, chief of surgical services, "instruments have been added over the years as new instruments become available, but seldom are instruments removed from the tray."

After analysis, the range for unused instruments was found to be 22 to 50 percent. For certain procedures, unused instruments reached as high as 88 percent.

16 RPIWs Bring a Bounty of Improvements

Sixteen RPIWs from 2004 to 2006 targeted the reduction of unused instruments and supplies across all surgical specialties. Standard work for this type of workshop guided each team. Scope and procedure/case types were selected approximately five weeks prior to the workshop week.

"The selection of projects is done using Patient Quantity Analysis data on supply usage for the previous 12 months," says Ted

Wegleitner, vice president for surgical services. "In other words, the highest volume cases were standardized first. Currently, nearly 85 percent of the case volume has been reached through an instrument-standardization RPIW."

During the RPIW preparation weeks, data were collected on instruments—used versus unused—by following the instrument trays after surgery. Cycle times for tray processing and supply picks were measured and unique instrument and supply adds (those instruments added to a standard case cart by surgeon request) for each individual surgeon were evaluated for the frequency of their use and commonalities between surgeons within each specialty.

Along with the team lead and sub-team lead, the RPIW team members typically included a circulating nurse and a surgical scrub technician from the specialty. They were notified of their partici-pation 4 to 6 weeks prior to the workshop week. Their familiarity with the procedure and their knowledge of each individual surgeon's preference made them invaluable in the analysis of both supplies and instruments. A physician from the specialty was also identified as a content expert to the team. The physician's role is critical to the suc-cess of the standardization projects.

The most important element for each of these projects is a meeting with the surgeons during the RPIW week, where the rec-ommended reductions are clearly displayed with actual trays, sup-plies, and sutures. The surgeons are then allowed to evaluate the reductions with the scrub tech and circulating nurse. Often, this meeting stimulated discussion between surgeons regarding best practice. This further promoted standardization.

Substantial Results

So, what was the result of all the RPIWs?

- The number of instruments in inventory was cut from 2.7 million to 1.6 million, a 41 percent reduction.

Figure 12.1

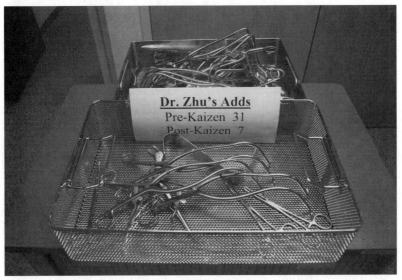

**Before-and-after RPIW photograph of the "add tray"—surgical instruments pro-
vided in addition to those on a standard surgical cart—provided to one of Park
Nicollet's surgeons.**

Source: Park Nicollet Health Services. Used with permission.

• The number of adds decreased from 349,000 to 120,000, a 66
percent reduction.

Although surgical services has not specifically measured the
cost savings from reduced handling of instruments, it estimates
that nearly six hours per day are eliminated. This amounts to .75
FTE. Figures 12.1 and 12.2 demonstrate visually the effect of the
RPIW.

Other *Kaizen* Activities at PNHS Surgery

Although the standardization of surgical case carts has been a
noteworthy success, surgical services has achieved other goals
through Lean:

Figure 12.2

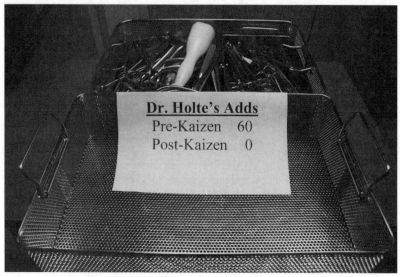

Dr. Holte's Adds
Pre-Kaizen   60
Post-Kaizen   0

Before-and-after photograph showing how an RPIW totally eliminated additional instruments provided to one surgeon.

Source: Park Nicollet Health Services. Used with permission.

- Through preoperative preparation (e.g., consent form signed, patient history reviewed, physical performed, lab tests reviewed, bathroom visit taken care of) delays in the operating room have been reduced.
- By improving the flow from pre-op to the operating room, a recent RPIW demonstrated a 10- to 12-minute reduction in room-turnover time. Patient lead time through the entire surgery experience also has been reduced.
- Leveling production (*heijunka*) of surgery schedules by day of week has been implemented to make better use of the facility and staff with the goal of performing the same number of surgical cases each day. This production-leveling effort will significantly reduce the stress on support functions, such as the instrument-processing room and materials management, as well as the difficult staffing demands on peak-volume days.

Growing Pains

Wegleitner and Dr. Connelly admit that the journey to Lean in surgery has been difficult at times.

"Looking back," says Dr. Connelly, "we didn't engage surgeons enough. They tend to learn by the Socratic method. They demand transparency with Lean, visibility of both the successes and the failure. As we get more of them involved, resistance goes down."

"Every person has his or her own comfort zone for change," adds Wegleitner. "Just the other day at an RPIW report-out, a general surgeon went out of his way to tell the audience that one of his own ideas didn't work. This shows we're catching on to the idea of 'failing forward.' It is an important Lean principle."

Wegleitner also says it can be difficult to tread the fine line between the role of the operational managers and supervisors and that of the KOT. "We're working to create an environment where operational leaders feel supported by the KOT and the communication is open and fearless."

As more and more staff become certified in Lean and/or participate in RPIWs, Wegleitner and Dr. Connelly can feel the momentum swinging strongly in Lean's favor. "Lean is taking hold much more now than six months ago," says Dr. Connelly. "We're definitely on an uptrend."

CHAPTER TAKEAWAYS

- Seven RPIWs over a two-year span enabled Park Nicollet's primary care clinics to reduce patient rooming time, drastically cut patient rooming defects, and reduce one nurse's walking distance by 65 percent.
- Additionally, by printing lab results directly to individual departments at each clinic site, manual driving of reports to clinics was cut from 62,120 miles a year to zero.
- Applying Lean to care provided to Type II diabetes patients

(Continued on following page)

(Continued from previous page)

enabled the primary care system to cut the lead time from a blood draw to notifying the patient of results by 99 percent, so that the clinician had the results during the office visit and not afterward. Also, better pre-visit planning enabled primary care to more than double the percentage of Type II diabetes patients receiving optimally managed care.

- Within medical subspecialties, a series of 12 RPIWs were conducted to improve the endoscopy center. In addition to many other positive results, patient throughput was increased dramatically and the lead time from specimen collection to notifying patients of results was cut by 50 percent.
- Two 3Ps resulted in the design of a new facility opened in February of 2007 that is able to further increase the number of endoscopic procedures and clinic visits per day.
- The application of Lean to surgical case carts has led to a decrease in the number of surgical instruments in inventory from 2.7 million to 1.6 million (a reduction of 41 percent) and a 66 percent reduction in the number of surgical adds (those instruments added to a standard case cart by surgeon request).

Afterword

Well, that's it. That's my story of Lean in healthcare up to the present, at least my version. There's more I could tell you about Lean, of course. There are additional tools available that I haven't mentioned, but maybe that's another book and another time. But I've covered the main things: the principles, the processes, and the major tools and methods.

Hopefully, by now you've gotten these messages:

1. Lean works if you really work to understand it.
2. It takes guts, commitment, leadership, time, and persistence.
3. You can do it if you lead it yourself; otherwise, forget it.

Admittedly, Lean isn't easy. Few things in life that bring great rewards are. Neither is it impossible. Toyota has done it. Boeing has done it. Virginia Mason Medical Center and Park Nicollet Health Services are doing it. And all are much better off for taking up the challenge.

What I've tried to present in this book, to the best of my ability, is a basic understanding of what Lean production is, as well as a step-by-step process for applying it to your healthcare organization.

Although there are many elements and layers to Lean, the basic approach isn't that hard to understand and apply:

1. Leadership commits.
2. Leadership leads.
3. Leaders are trained.
4. Leaders are certified.
5. A Lean infrastructure is built.
6. Model lines are selected.
7. *Takt* time (demand rate) is gauged and leveled production (*heijunka*) is applied.
8. Standard operations, based on just in time, are implemented.
9. RPIWs ("*kaizen* events") are conducted.
10. RPIW/*kaizen* successes are duplicated and extended throughout the organization.
11. *Kaizen* (continuous incremental improvement) becomes a way of life.
12. Patients get world-class healthcare.

There is not much variation in the ordering of these steps. They are the basics for success. All who've embarked on this journey have had to start somewhere—that somewhere being whatever state of repair or disrepair their organization is at the present time. The good news is that you don't have to start from scratch. There are people out there who can help you.

As I've stressed in the book, the assistance of a Japanese master (*sensei*) or a consultant trained by a *sensei* is recommended. You need to go as far upstream as you can—in other words, find those who have learned Lean either directly from Taiichi Ohno or those who are the students of the students of Ohno.

At Boeing, we went directly to Shingijutsu Company, Ltd. The founder, Yoshiki Iwata, was an original member of the Toyota Autonomous Study Group (a project team comprised of Toyota's subsidiary companies). This study group first developed Toyota's

Lean production practices (the *kaizen* system). The study activities enabled Iwata to contribute in establishing the Toyota Production System (TPS) as a primary pupil of Ohno (an originator of the TPS concept). Iwata founded Shingijutsu to promote this *kaizen* system throughout the world. Shingijutsu brought the *kaizen* system to a wide range of industries, including automotive, electronics, and printing.

Yoshiki Iwata passed away in 2001, and Chihiro Nakao, a former vice president, successfully took over Iwata's position. However, in 2003 differing visions of the future of Shingijutsu and about its marketing strategy arose within Shingijutsu. At that time, Iwata's daughter, Kumi Iwata Otake, along with Senji Niwa and other senior consultants, decided to form a new company, Shingijutsu Global Consulting Company, to preserve and develop Yoshiki Iwata's original business concept.

Though Shingijutsu Global Consulting Company is still a fledgling company, its founders' experience and knowledge of the *kaizen* and *kanban* systems were nurtured and cultivated under the leadership of Yoshiki Iwata himself, and the company is dedicated to developing and promoting his vision. To that end, Shingijutsu Global Consulting Company recently opened a U.S. subsidiary in Bellevue, Washington, to better serve clients in the United States and Europe. They can be contacted at:

Shingijutsu Global Consulting USA, Inc.,
10900 N.E. 4th Street, Suite 1915
Bellevue, WA 98004
Phone: 425.451.8651
Fax: 425.451.8652
E-mail: office@shingijutsu-global.com

If you want help from an American consulting firm in implementing Lean, I strongly recommend that the firm's Lean consultants meet the following criteria:

1. A minimum of 20 years' experience in a line-management position responsible for a budget,
2. References that attest to their success in consulting a minimum of five years on the "pure" Shingijutsu method as explained in detail in this book, particularly Chapter 4, where I talk about the "Lean House,"
3. An additional minimum of five years' experience as head of a *Kaizen* Promotion Office (KPO),
4. Certificates of completion from Shingijutsu in Japan for the following training courses and seminars: *Gemba Kaizen*, KPO Super Flow, *Kanban*, 3P (production preparation process), and
5. Have served as a team leader on a minimum of 50 *kaizen* events (RPIWs) and five 3P events.

Good luck.

John Black

Appendix

VIRGINIA MASON MEDICAL CENTER PHYSICIAN COMPACT

Organization's Responsibilities	Physician's Responsibilities
Foster Excellence	*Focus on Patients*
• Recruit and train superior physicians and staff	• Practice state-of-the-art, quality medicine
• Support career development and professional satisfaction	• Encourage patient involvement in care and treatment decisions
• Acknowledge contributions to patient care and the organization	• Achieve and maintain optimal patient access
• Create opportunities to participate in or support research	• Insist on seamless service
Listen and Communicate	*Collaborate on Care Delivery*
• Share information regarding strategic intent, organizational priorities, and business decisions	• Include staff, physicians, and management on team
• Offer opportunities for constructive dialogue	• Treat all members with respect
• Provide regular, written evaluation and feedback	• Demonstrate the highest levels of ethical and professional conduct
	• Behave in a manner consistent with group goals
	• Participate in or support teaching

Educate
- Support and facilitate teaching, GME, and CME
- Provide information and tools necessary to improve practice

Listen and Communicate
- Communicate clinical information in clear, timely manner
- Request information, resources needed to provide care consistent with VMMC goals
- Provide and accept feedback

Reward
- Provide clear compensation with internal and market consistency, aligned with organizational goals
- Create an environment that supports teams and individuals

Take Ownership
- Implement VMMC-accepted clinical standards of care
- Participate in and support group decisions
- Focus on the economic aspects of the practice

Lead
- Manage and lead organization with integrity and accountability

Change
- Embrace innovation and continuous improvement
- Participate in necessary organizational change

Glossary

3P—Production preparation process. The purpose of 3P is to structure a defect-free, world-class quality of care that can be delivered at the required patient-demand volume (*takt* time) and in the correct timing (just in time) with simple and defect-free processes. The focus is the patient and the challenge is to start "with a blank sheet of paper" (no preconceptions or limitations). Adopt the mind of a 13-year-old.

5S—A key consideration in Lean operations is maintaining a clean, well-organized workplace. To do so, Lean employs what is known as a 5S process. The elements of this process are:

> **Sort.** Separate the necessary from the unnecessary by removing superfluous tools, equipment, and procedures from the workplace.
>
> **Simplify.** Put everything in its place and organize material according to how frequently it is used, preferably with the help of visual aids.
>
> **Sweep.** Visually identify potential problems and deal with unsafe conditions or damaged equipment early in the process.

Standardize. Define how a task should best be done and effectively communicate this to everyone involved. Document process changes as they occur.

Self-Discipline. Ensure that all housekeeping policies are adhered to by everyone. (This usually paves the way for success in other quality-improvement efforts.)

5 whys process—Taiichi Ohno's practice of asking "why" five times whenever a problem was encountered in order to identify the root cause of the problem so that effective countermeasures could be developed and implemented.

7-7 rule—The requirement that managers have at least seven managers reporting to them.

Anchor draggers—Those managers or other employees who won't give new ideas a fair trial.

Andon—Visual control device, usually a light, that alerts supervisors to factory floor needs or problems.

Brownfield—An established facility or process. Contrast with Greenfield.

Cascade Scheduling—Staggering start times for patients and staff.

Catch-ball process—Where goals are proposed and discussed by people all the way down and up the chain of command.

Cell—Work area.

Continuous flow production—An approach to production that stresses little or no in-process inventory. The eight conditions to establish this approach are: (1) one-piece flow, (2) lay out equipment according to the sequence of processes, (3) synchronization, (4) multi-process operations, (5) training of multi-process workers, (6) standing while working, (7) make equipment compact, and (8) create U-shaped manufacturing cells.

Cycle time—The amount of time it takes to complete a task or process.

Even flow—Processes working in concert with each other to prevent bottlenecks.

Flow—The progressive achievement of tasks along the value stream so that a service proceeds from request to delivery smoothly and efficiently, without stoppages and waste. Flow is a very important concept in Lean production.

Gemba—Where the work gets done, e.g., the factory or hospital floor.

Gemba kaizen—Training that occurs on the factory floor via real-life problem solving.

Global Production System (GPS, also known as the Lean House)—A generic and graphic representation of the Toyota Production System (TPS, or Lean).

Greenfield—A new facility or process. Contrast with Brownfield.

Heijunka—Also known as leveled production, scheduling products and services in such a way as to eliminate bottlenecks and maximize throughput.

Hoshin kanri—Mangagement policy. A strategic decision-making tool for a firm's executive team that focuses resources on the critical initiatives necessary to accomplish the business objectives of the firm. The selected objectives are translated into specific services and deployed down to the implementation level in the firm.

Infrastructure—See "Lean infrastructure."

Inventory—Inventory is all physical goods on hand needed in the provision of services to the customer, or patient.

Jidoka—The intelligent use of both people and technology, with the ability (even obligation) to stop any process at the first sign of an abnormality. In other words, a system that keeps the patient safe, not gets him harmed or killed.

Just-in-time (JIT) production (healthcare)—Consistently delivering only the healthcare service that is needed, in just the required amount, where it is needed, and when it is needed. Virtually no inventory is required.

Kaikaku—Broadscale and radical improvement. Apply *kaikaku*—specifically 3P (production preparation process)—to powerfully reconfigure the entire value stream.

Kaizen—Continuous incremental improvement.

Kaizen **event**—See "Rapid Process Improvement Workshop."

Kaizen **Promotion Office (KPO)**—The purpose of the KPO is to promote and manage all improvement activities in the system.

Kanban—A way of automatically signaling when new parts, supplies, or services are needed. In Japanese, *kanban* means sign, signboard, doorplate, poster, billboard, or card, but is taken more broadly to mean any kind of signal.

Kit—All materials needed at point of use put in a single container.

Lead time—The time to complete a patient-care event, including processing time and waiting time—in other words, it's the time from when the patient requests a service until it is provided.

Lean accounting—The authors' term for the merging of Lean management principles, processes, and practices with the budgeting ideas of management experts Robin Fraser and Jeremy Hope as set forth in their 2003 book *Beyond Budgeting: How Managers Can Break Free from the Annual Performance Trap*. The major difference between Lean accounting and traditional budgeting is that fixed financial targets are replaced with targets based on key performance indicators. In this way, the budget process works to improve performance on a continual basis.

Lean depth study—A hard, objective look at the potential waste in the structure of the chain of command.

Lean House—See "Global Production System."

Lean infrastructure—The Lean infrastructure includes a compelling vision, an organizational structure, a strategic plan, a management system, and a Lean knowledge base of Lean leaders, educated employees, and consultants. Without an adequate Lean infrastructure, Lean implementation cannot succeed (or fully succeed).

Lean production (or simply Lean)—Lean production, based on the Toyota Production System, is a term applied to the production methods pioneered in Japan after World War II by Kiichiro Toyoda and Taiichi Ohno of the Toyota Motor Corporation. Lean is a production strategy in which all parts of the production system are focused on eliminating waste while continuously increasing the percentage of value-added work. The term was coined by John Krafcik of the International Motor Vehicle Program at Massachussets Institute of Technology. It was first publicized in the book *The Machine that Changed the World: The Story of Lean Production* by James P. Womak, Daniel T. Jones, and Daniel Roos.

Lean thinking—Cutting waste by half over and over again.

Low-hanging fruit—The easiest improvement opportunities.

Mistake-proofing—A defect-prevention system that builds into a production or service process devices or procedures that make mistakes impossible.

Model line—Lean implementation in one part of an organization.

Monument—Immovable piece of equipment or furnishing.

Muda—Waste, meaning any activity, service, or supply that consumes time, money, and other resources, but creates no value.

Muri—Unreasonableness.

One-piece flow—In one-piece flow, all equipment, other supplies, and information are physically grouped together to enable one person to perform all the steps necessary to complete a process or action. The opposite of batching work.

Operational availability—The availability of healthcare equipment when needed.

Par level—In *kanban*, the level of supplies and inventory considered prudent to maintain on hand.

Patient-procedure/quantity analysis (PQA)—Adapted from product-quantity analysis in a manufacturing setting. In healthcare, PQA helps line up processes for flow production by grouping patients and procedures for cellular (work area) service.

Patient Safety Alert (PSA)—Virginia Mason Medical Center's version of stop the line.

Point of use (medication)—Medication storage is located where patients receive treatment.

Pokayoke—The Japanese term for a mistake-proofing device or procedure to prevent defects.

Process—A series of individual operations required to create a design, completed order, or product.

Pull production—A system where parts, supplies, information, and services are pulled by internal and external customers exactly when they are needed.

Rapid Process Improvement Workshop (RPIW; also known as *kaizen* event)—A team of people who do the work, fully engaged in a rigorous and disciplined five-day process, using the tools of Lean to achieve immediate results in the elimination of waste.

Sensei—A personal teacher with the mastery of a body of knowledge, in this case Lean production.

Sketching—A technique of Lean where participants observe and sketch Lean in action. See "Super flow."

Sleeping inventory—Inventory that has largely been forgotten.

Spaghetti chart—A diagram of patient and staff flow.

Standard operation—The normal steps and time required to perform a specific operation.

Standard operations—Working to customer requirements of *takt* time, standard work, and standard work-in-process.

Standard work—A prescribed, repeatable sequence of steps (or actions) that balances people's work to *takt* time.

Standard work-in-process (SWIP)—In healthcare, the amount of work-in-process inventory on the floor to provide patient care for the day.

Standard work sheet—A document identifying the steps necessary to complete a task, who should perform each step, and the reasonable (repeatable) amount of time to complete each step.

Stop the line—Where any staff member can stop any process or procedure if that staff member believes proceeding would adversely affect patient safety or efficient operations. An element of *jidoka*.

Super flow—Training in Japan where participants are taken to a variety of world-class manufacturing plants, including Toyota factories, to observe Lean in action and practice sketching the seven factory flows: people, information, equipment, raw materials, parts (sub-assemblies), final product, and engineering (gauges, tools, fixtures, and integration of all three).

***Takt* time**—Production time aligned with the rate of demand. In healthcare, the time it should take to provide a service to one patient based on overall rate of demand from all patients. For example, imagine that overall patient demand—or market demand—is for 40 patient visits per healthcare provider in an eight-hour day (480 minutes). Let's say 60 minutes of any provider's day is taken up with breaks, meetings, and other planned time when she is not available for patient care. That leaves 420 minutes. To meet patient demand then, the provider would need to complete a patient visit every 10.5 minutes (420 minutes ÷ 40 patients) to meet the market demand. This is *takt* time. *Takt* time makes leveled production (*heijunka*) possible.

Throughput time—The time required for a service to proceed from request to delivery.

Toyota Production System (TPS)—See "Lean production."

Value—The patient's perception of how a service provided matches what he desires in terms of quality, price, time spent, and other factors.

Value stream—The specific activities required to provide a specific service to the patient.

Value-stream map—A pictorial representation of the steps in a value stream, either as a current or future (desired) state.

Walk time—Time spent walking from one location to another.

"Wash your hands" *kaizen* event—Where participants in Lean education observe and participate in an RPIW on the factory floor.

Waste—See "*Muda.*"

World class—Waste free.

World-class management system (WCMS)—A management system consisting of three elements: daily management, management by policy (MBP), and cross-functional management.

Acknowledgments

First of all, I want to thank my agent and long time friend, Bill Christopher—the agent for my first title, *A World Class Production System*—who told me I needed to write this book. Bill is a retired business executive, consultant, owner of a literary agency, and author who has written twelve major pieces of work on management. His latest book is *Holistic Management: Managing What Matters for Company Success.* Bill and I became friends in the mid 1980s when I was working with the American Productivity and Quality Center in Houston, Texas, while also employed at Boeing.

I also want to thank Audrey Kaufman, acquisitions manager for Health Administration Press, who had the faith in me and this project to commit her company to this book's publication. I hope this work has exceeded her expectations and those of you, the reader.

I also owe a debt of gratitude to Bruce Gissing, retired executive vice president of Boeing. His leadership in getting all of Boeing's top executives to visit Japan in the early 1990s began that company's transformation toward operating according to world-class principles and practices, as well as implementing the Toyota Production System.

Carolyn Corvi, vice president and general manager of Airplane Programs at Boeing Commercial Airplanes and a board member at Virginia Mason Medical Center in Seattle, has been steadfast in her support of my efforts. Her leadership in promoting the Toyota Production System in healthcare has provided a shining example of commitment and dedication.

I'm also grateful to my Japanese teachers, *senseis* Yoshiki Iwata, chairman and founder of Shingijutsu Global Consulting, Ltd. (now deceased), and Yashuro Nakao, president of Shingijutsu Global Consulting, Ltd.—both former members of Taiichi Ohno's *Kaizen* Promotion Office at Toyota. They showed faith in my abilities and invited me to become a member of Shingijutsu's consulting team. This helped prepare me for consulting when I retired from Boeing in 1999.

Of course, I owe a special debt of gratitude to my wife, Joanne Poggetti, not only for her emotional support during the writing of this book, but who, as a protégé of Dr. W. Edwards Deming, taught me much about healthcare consulting. My education began when I assisted Joanne in preparing the first team ever of healthcare executives to attend a Shingijutsu *gemba kaizen* (factory-floor improvement experience) in the early 1990s.

I must also thank my Japanese business partners at Shingijutsu Global Consulting: Senji Niwa, chairman of the board; Kumi Iwata Otake, president and CEO; and Takashi Shimura, Katsuya Koide, and Takeshi Iwata, executive consultants. They have provided consulting support to my clients, both in Japan and in the United States. Both Shingijutsu Global Consulting and Shingijutsu USA have hosted hundreds of John Black and Associates (JBA) healthcare clients in training seminars in Japan since 2001.

I also owe a debt of gratitude to Alberto Galgano, chairman and CEO of Galgano Group in Milan, Italy. We've partnered on many projects in his country. His many books on Lean, as well as trips to Japan with Shingijutsu, have benefited hundreds of his clients in Italy and throughout Europe. I consider Alberto the Dr. Deming of Europe.

On the American side, some former colleges of mine at Boeing, who later became JBA team members, were instrumental in bringing the Japanese method to healthcare and deserve special mention: Mark Barnett (formerly with Boeing); Bill Creel of William A. Creel and Associates (retired from Boeing); and Jon F. Sutter, consultant (also formerly with Boeing). Special thanks are owed as well to Bill Sandras of Productivity Centers International (formerly a Hewlett

Packard employee), now a John Black associate helping lead the Park Nicollet "Leadership Fellows" Program. All of these people continue to spend hundreds of hours in the air and on the ground making a profound difference in how healthcare is delivered.

Several managers of Genie-Terex of Redmond, Washington, have also from time to time supported JBA's healthcare clients as consultants: Paul Caldarazzo, Dean Wisler, Bruce Lawson, Reid Stromberg, and Brent Williams. Bruce, Reid, Dean, and Brent were former Boeing Production System specialists.

Finally, David Miller, co-writer and retired director of Executive Communications for Weyerhaeuser, has been invaluable in his edits, rewrites, and wise counsel in getting this book completed.

Index

GPS. *See* Global Production System
Greenfield, 71

H

Hampson, Neil, 174–175, 178, 179, 181–182, 187
Hartquist, Beth, 207, 209–211
Harvard School of Public Health, 14–15
Health unit coordinator (HUC), 214
Hebeler, Bud, 32
Heijunka
  application, 169, 215, 222
  clinician flow and, 113
  definition, 46
  explanation, 47–48
  importance of, 59, 139, 142
  Lean House, 45–48, 49
  model service line and, 56, 64
  reorder point, 133
  use in training, 95
Herman, John, 192
Hetzel, Joe, 133, 134–138, 140, 144
Hope, Jeremy, 66
HUC. *See* Health unit coordinator

I

Inelastic demand, 37
Information flow, 121–123
Infrastructure. *See* Lean infrastructure
Institute of Medicine, 14
Internal leaders, 65
Inventory, 19–20
Iwata, Takeshi, 130, 133, 143
Iwata, Yoshiki, 35, 44, 226–227

J

Jacobs, Andrew, 166, 168, 173
Japan study trip, 32–34, 37, 58, 90, 94, 97–98, 103, 155, 156, 159, 160
Jefferson, Thomas, 28
Jidoka
  application, 156, 169

continuous improvement cycle of, 55
definition, 29, 59
equipment flow application, 124
Lean production and, 9
Lean House, 45, 46, 48, 49, 55
patient flow and, 108
purpose, 48
use in training, 95
JIT. *See* Just-in-time production
Johnson, Todd, 138, 140, 141
Jones, Daniel T., 4, 95
Juran, Joseph, 30, 32
Just-in-time delivery, 119
Just-in-time (JIT) production
  definition, 59
  jidoka and, 48–49
  kanban and, 29, 130, 131, 141, 143, 144
  Lean and, 9
  Lean House component, 45, 46, 48, 55
  supply flow, 119

K

Kaikaku
  definition, 64
  example, 72–75
kaizen and, 64, 69–71, 85, 165
Kaiser Family Foundation
  healthcare premiums, 15
  healthcare quality poll, 15
  medical errors survey, 14–15
Kaizen
  career ladder, 198
  definition of, 6
  involvement in, 11, 24, 128, 198
  kaikaku and, 64, 69–71, 85, 165
  leader, 65, 91–98
  masters, 99–100
  path, 75, 76
Kaizen event (Rapid Process Improvement Workshop)

movement waste, 21
Neurology Clinic, 23
paradigm shifts, 151
patient flow, 107, 109
patient safety alerts, 21–22, 48, 169–170
physician compact, 90, 229–230
process engineering flow, 125–126, 126–127
process waste, 23
program audit, 160–161
reaffirmation, 154–155
redundancy, 18–19
results, 172
stand-up meeting, 82
strategic plan, 42, 43
supply flow, 118
transformational process, 159–160
wait time, 19
Virginia Mason Production System (VMPS), 155
Visibility room, 81, 82
Vision, 43–44
Visit planning, 208–210
Visual control device (*andon*), 22
Visual displays, 173
Visual management boards, 210–211
VMMC. *See* Virginia Mason Medical Center
VMPS. *See* Virginia Mason Production System, 155
VSM. *See* Value-stream map

W

Wait time
waste in, 19
definition, 21
Walk time, 213, 216
"Wash your hands" *kaizen* event, 63, 97
Waste
causes of, 16–17
of defective products, 21–22

definition, 13, 14–16, 25
effects of, 14–16
in healthcare, 14, 17–24
identification of, 24
of movement, 20–21
of overproduction, 18–19
in processing, 23–24
of stock on hand, 19–20
of time on hand, 19
in transportation, 22–23
reduction, 7
types of, 9, 25
Waste-elimination strategy, 64
WCC. *See* World Class Competitiveness course
WCMS. *See* World-class management system
Wegleitner, Ted, 219–220, 223
Wessner, David, 58, 100, 192, 196, 198, 199–200, 201, 202, 203
Whitney, Eli, 28
Womack, James P., 4, 95
Work areas, 113
Workload, 215
Workplace
kaizen events, 64
organization, 53–54
World class, 9, 32–34
World Class Competitiveness (WCC) course, 34
World Class Production System, A, 95
World Health Organization, 16
World-class management system (WCMS)
elements, 77–81
implementation, 65–66, 80

About the Authors

JOHN BLACK

In his career with the Boeing Company, John Black was the first to introduce the ideas of quality gurus Dr. W. Edwards Deming and Dr. Joseph Juran to the company. He went on to gain management's commitment to the Toyota Production System (Lean).

Since retiring from Boeing and founding his own consulting firm, John Black and Associates (www.johnblackandassociates.com), Black has developed broad experience helping healthcare organizations implement Lean operations. Clients include Virginia Mason Medical Center in Seattle, Park Nicollet Health Services in Minneapolis, and Premera Blue Shield of Lynnwood, Washington.

Black's first book, *A World Class Production System*, has been updated and greatly expanded to reflect his additional decade of experience with the concepts and clients successfully executing them. The revised version, *A Lean, World-Class Production System*, is expected from Industrial Press in late 2008.

DAVID MILLER

David Miller is a former executive speechwriter and communications director at a *Fortune* 500 firm. He also has published two novels and numerous articles for corporate and non-corporate publications.